121 CARDS
for All Occasions™

Edited by Vicki Blizzard

Annie's Attic®

121 CARDS
for All Occasions™

To me, a handcrafted card says that someone really cares about me—enough to spend time creating a card that is personal and unique.

We asked our designers to come up with ideas for cards to take you from January

through December, and every-thing in between, including a few rather unique holidays, such as National Pig Day (March 1). They've done a great job!

Take out your card-making supplies and get started. Treat those people you care about to handmade expressions of your love—cards you've created especially for them!

Warm regards,

Vicki Blizzard

CONTENTS

Staff
Editor: Vicki Blizzard
Associate Editor: Tanya Fox
Copy Editors: Michelle Beck, Conor Allen
Technical Editor: Brooke Smith
Technical Artist: Brooke Smith
Graphic Arts Supervisor: Ronda Bechinski
Graphic Artist: Pam Gregory
Photography: Christena Green
Photo Stylist: Tammy Nussbaum

Annie's Attic®

306 East Parr Road, Berne, IN 46711
©2005 Annie's Attic

TOLL-FREE ORDER LINE or to request
a free catalog (800) 582-6643
Customer Service (800) 282-6643,
Fax (800) 882-6643
Pattern Services (260) 589-4000, ext. 333

Visit www.AnniesAttic.com

121 Cards for All Occasions is published by Annie's Attic, 306 East Parr Road, Berne, IN 46711, telephone (260) 589-4000. Printed in USA. Copyright © 2005 Annie's Attic. RETAILERS: If you would like to carry this pattern book or any other Annie's Attic publications, call the Wholesale Department at Annie's Attic to set up a direct account: (903) 636-4303. Toll-free order line or to request a free catalog (800) LV-ANNIE (800-582-6643). Customer Service: (800) AT-ANNIE (800-282-6643), Fax (800) 882-6643. Also, request a complete listing of publications available from Annie's Attic. Visit www.AnniesAttic.com.

ISBN: 1-59635-002-4
Library of Congress: 2004110067
1 2 3 4 5 6 7 8 9

New Year's Peace

Design by LENAE GERIG, *courtesy of Hot Off The Press*

MATERIALS

White card stock
2 varying light blue
  patterned papers
Christmas sentiment
  quotes
Pre-embossed silver
  snowflake image
2 mini pewter brads
Coordinating blue ribbon
Light blue chalk
$\frac{1}{16}$-inch hole punch
Adhesive foam squares
Glue stick
Computer font

Cut a 5 x 10-inch piece of white card stock; score and fold in half. Glue a piece of patterned paper to front of card; trim edges even with card. Cut a 4 x 5-inch strip of different patterned paper; glue to center of card and trim edges even.

Tear out desired Christmas quote; apply chalk to the edges. Punch a hole on the left and right side; insert brads. Adhere quote to card. Cut two 3-inch lengths of ribbon and wrap the center of each around a brad. Glue down the ends and trim ends even with card. Cut out the pre-embossed snowflake; adhere to card using adhesive foam squares.

Cut a 3½ x 5-inch strip of patterned paper; adhere inside card. Tear out another card quote; apply chalk where desired. Adhere to paper strip inside. ◼

SOURCES: Papers, sentiment quotes, pre-embossed image, brads and ribbon from Hot Off The Press; chalk from Craf-T Products.

Happy New Year

Design by LENAE GERIG, *courtesy of Hot Off The Press*

MATERIALS

5 x 6½-inch blank
    white card
Clear vellum
Burgundy striped
    patterned paper
Burgundy with gold script
    patterned paper
Burgundy blank tag
Burgundy "Happy
    Holidays" tag
Word embellishments
Burgundy ribbon
Mini gold brad
Gold gel pen
Ruler
Mini adhesive dots
Craft glue

Glue a piece of burgundy striped paper to front of card; trim edges even with card. ***Note:*** *Stripes should run vertically.* Cut a 3 x 6½-inch strip of burgundy with gold script paper. Using a ruler and a gold gel pen, draw a line of gold along long edges of strip. Glue the strip ½ inch from card fold.

Cut a 1½ x 6½-inch strip of vellum; place a line of glue down the center and adhere to card referring to photo for placement. Cut a 6½-inch length of ribbon and adhere to vellum covering line of glue.

Glue "Happy Holidays" tag toward top of ribbon; make a bow with remaining ribbon and adhere to tag. Attach "Happy New Year" word embellishments underneath tag.

For the inside, cut two 1½ x 6½-inch strips of burgundy striped paper and one 3¼ x 6½-inch strip of burgundy with gold script paper. Apply a line of gold ink to the long edges of the gold script paper. Adhere striped pieces even against the inside edges of the card, one on the right side and one on the left; adhere remaining piece of paper down the center. Cut out blank tag and insert brad. Attach desired word embellishment on tag and adhere to inside bottom of card. ■

SOURCES: Papers, vellum, tags, brads, ribbon and word embellishments from Hot Off The Press; adhesive dots from Glue Dots.

Copper Medallions

Design by S A N D R A   G R A H A M   S M I T H

CARD

Fold gray card stock in half. Cut a 3¾ x 5-inch piece of dark blue card stock; using stencil brush, apply platinum silver ink over entire front side. Once dry, use decorative punch to embellish each corner; adhere to front of card. Attach a copper eyelet in each corner.

Cut a 3½ x 3¼-inch piece of dark blue card stock. Using platinum silver ink, stamp shadow square image four times onto card stock with even spacing between each image; glue piece to card.

Using clear embossing ink, stamp snowflake image six times onto dark blue card stock. Emboss all six images with copper embossing powder. Cut out each snowflake square; center and glue one in each of the stamped shadow square images on card.

Use a craft knife to cut out the center of one of the remaining snowflake images; discard center and adhere border on top of last snowflake image diagonally. Mount to center of card using adhesive foam dots.

ENVELOPE

Using clear embossing ink, stamp snowflake image six times onto dark blue card stock. Emboss each image with copper embossing powder. Cut out each snowflake square; cut out the centers of two of the images.

Glue one complete snowflake square to black flap; glue three complete snowflake squares to left side of envelope with even spacing. Adhere one of the cut borders diagonally to the glued middle image. Glue remaining cut border to upper right side of envelope. ■

SOURCES: Shadow rubber stamp from Hero Arts.

MATERIALS

- 2 (8½ x 11-inch sheets) dark blue card stock
- 5½ x 8½-inch gray card stock
- 4¾ x 5¾-inch white envelope
- Platinum silver ink pad
- Clear embossing ink pad
- Copper embossing powder
- Decorative snowflake square rubber stamp
- Shadow square rubber stamp
- Small decorative corner punch
- 4 (⅛-inch) copper eyelets
- Eyelet punch and hammer
- Stencil brush
- Heat embossing tool
- Glue stick
- Adhesive foam dots
- Scissors
- Craft knife
- Cutting mat

Delicate Snowflakes DIAGRAMS ON PAGE 89

Design by BARBARA GREVE

MATERIALS

5 x 6½-inch white card

5 x 7-inch white beveled
    mat

140-lb watercolor paper

1⅛-inch diameter
    snowflake foam stamp

Acrylic paint: silver, gold,
    gray-blue, light blue
    and opalescent blue

Stamping medium

Light blue and dark blue
    4-ply embroidery
    threads

Sewing needle

Small sea sponge

Salt

Tracing paper

Graphite transfer paper

Pencil with a flat-ended
    eraser

Foam brush

Mounting tape

Fabric adhesive

Paper plate

Lightly draw a 7 x 9-inch rectangle on watercolor paper; dampen the area with water and randomly sponge gray-blue paint onto area. Sprinkle a small amount of salt randomly onto the painted area. Once dry, brush off salt and cut out rectangle.

Copy the snowflake pattern onto tracing paper and transfer it to the watercolor paper using transfer paper. Using sewing needle and light blue thread, backstitch the outlines of two of the snowflakes. Use the dark blue thread to stitch the remaining two snowflakes; use French knots on the ends of the feathery snowflakes.

Mix equal amounts of stamping medium and light blue acrylic paint; apply mixture to snowflake image and stamp randomly over stitched snowflakes. Mix equal amounts of stamping medium with light blue and gray-blue paints; apply mixture to pencil eraser and stamp randomly around snowflakes. Set aside to dry.

Use the sea sponge to apply silver paint to beveled mat; let dry. Repeat process with gold and then opalescent blue paints.

Adhere snowflake picture to front of card with fabric adhesive; use mounting tape to attach the beveled mat. ∎

SOURCES: Acrylic paints and stamping medium from DecoArt.

Let It Snow

Design by EMILY CALL,
courtesy of Stampin' Up!

Cut a 5½ x 8½-inch piece of brown flecked card stock; score and fold in half. Score a line ¾ inch from bottom; fold up to form a flap. Cut ½ inch off of flap; curl remaining edge slightly. Cut a strip of red card stock 5½ x 1¾ inches and adhere inside card behind flap keeping edges even with back of card.

Stamp small snowflake and small snowflake shadow images across center section of card using all three ink colors. Use light gray-blue ink to stamp larger snowflake shadow image onto a 2-inch square of cream flecked card stock; once dry, stamp medium snowflake image on top of shadow image using blue ink.

Sand the silver brad; attach to a piece of scrap paper and pound brad flat with hammer. Undo brad and attach to center of snowflake image. Adhere stamped square to red card stock; trim edges leaving a small border.

Use light gray-blue ink to stamp small snowflake shadow image randomly onto small tag; stamp "Let it snow!" on tag using red ink. Wrap silver wire around bottom of square; secure ends in back. Attach tag to square using an additional piece of wire; curl ends to secure. Referring to photo for placement, adhere square and tag to card using adhesive foam squares. ∎

SOURCES: Rubber stamps, card stock, tag, ink pads, brad, sanding block, wire and adhesive foam squares from Stampin' Up!.

MATERIALS

Card stock: brown flecked, red and cream flecked

Medium and small snowflake and snowflake shadow rubber stamps

Small alphabet rubber stamps

Ink pads: red, blue and light gray-blue

Small tag

Silver brad

Hammer

26-gauge silver wire

Sanding block

Adhesive foam squares

Scrap paper

Snow & Ice

Design by TRACI ARMBRUST, *courtesy of AccuCut*

MATERIALS

Large and small die-cut machines

Dies: card, envelope, small square and snowflake

Glitter flecked white card stock

Metallic silver card stock

Gold and silver flecked paper

Swirls texture plate

Stainless steel craft metal

¼-inch-wide silver wired ribbon

⁷⁄₁₆-inch clear flat-backed rhinestone

Small clear rhinestones

Glue pen

Glue stick

Double-sided tape

Using the large die-cut machine, cut out a card from gold and silver flecked paper; use the large die-cut machine to cut out an envelope from the same paper. Use small die-cut machine to cut a 3-inch square from silver card stock and a snowflake from glitter-flecked white card stock; glue snowflake to square. Adhere a small rhinestone on each end of snowflake and one large rhinestone in center of snowflake.

Cut a ⁵⁄₁₆-inch-wide strip of craft metal and use texture plate to add swirls onto strip. Use double-sided tape to adhere metal strip to card; trim ends even. Adhere snowflake square to center of card. Use glue stick to assemble envelope. ■

SOURCES: Die-cut machines and dies from AccuCut; card stock from Bazzill Basics; papers from The Paper Co. and The Paper Cut Inc.; rhinestones from Mrs. Grossman's.

Groundhog Greetings DIAGRAMS ON PAGE 89

Design by MARY AYRES

Cut black card stock 4 x 6 inches; punch photo slot in each corner. Cut cloud patterned paper 3½ x 5½ inches; cut sand patterned paper 1½ x 5½ inches and tear top edge. Glue sand rectangle to bottom of cloud rectangle lining up edges.

Using patterns provided, cut groundhog from light brown card stock with decorative-edge scissors. Use a craft sponge to apply brown ink to edges of groundhog. Referring to photo, assemble groundhog. Punch ⅛-inch holes for eyes; attach black eyelets. Glue button to muzzle; tie burlap strands into a bow and glue to left side of neck. Adhere groundhog to rectangle lining up bottom edges. Insert assembled rectangle into photo slots; apply a small amount of paper adhesive to secure.

Use a computer or hand-print "groundhog greetings" on vellum; tear a 1¼-inch-wide strip around words. Position strip diagonally across top right corner of card; tear vellum at top and side edges. Punch a ¹⁄₁₆-inch hole on each side; attach pewter brads. Write desired message on back of postcard with white gel pen. ■

SOURCES: Patterned papers from The Paper Loft; brads from Creative Impressions; Zip Dry paper adhesive from Beacon.

MATERIALS

Light brown and black
    card stock
Clear vellum
Sand patterned paper
Clouds patterned paper
Photo slot corner punch
Decorative-edge scissors
⅛- and ¹⁄₁₆-inch circle
    punches
2 burlap strands
⅝-inch flat black button
2 black round eyelets
2 pewter round brads
White gel pen
Brown ink pad
Craft sponge
Instant-dry paper adhesive
Computer font (optional)

Cherished Find

Design by STACEY WAKELIN

MATERIALS

3 large tags

Burgundy card stock

Patterned paper with
    printed words

Photo tabs

Assorted paper and metal
    word embellishments

Coordinating scrapbook
    stickers

29 inches hemp cord

2 decorative brads

Brown ink

Craft sponge

Adhesive foam dots

Glue stick

Using craft sponge, apply brown ink over entire surface of each tag. Once dry, lay the three tags side by side; place photo tabs along the inside seams to join them together. Turn the tags over and cut a strip of card stock approximately 3½ inches wide. Place hemp cord centered horizontally along the tags and adhere card stock on top of cord. Trim card stock even with edges; turn tags over.

Cut another piece of card stock the same size as previous piece; adhere to front of tags. Trim edges if needed. Tear a piece of patterned paper to fit onto front of tags; adhere and apply ink to paper. Embellish using metal words, stickers, brads, etc. Fold tags up like an accordion and use cord as a tie for card. ■

SOURCES: Paper embellishments and brads from Making Memories; metal embellishments from K&Company; stickers from Far & Away Scrapbooks; paper from 7 Gypsies.

Buttoned-Up Love

Designs by SHARON REINHART

Cut two pieces of pink card stock, one measuring 2⅛ x 2⅞ inches and the other measuring 1¾ x 3½ inches. Center and tape brass stencil right side up to the first piece; turn piece over and place onto a light source with stencil sandwiched between paper and light source. Rub a piece of wax paper over pink card stock.

Use stylus to trace design by gently pressing into edge of motifs; trace around perimeter of stencil and remove paper from stencil. Trim around outer edge of image using decorative-edge scissors. Lightly sand embossed motif and edges.

Thread sewing needle with metallic pink thread and stitch through both buttons three to four times; secure on back sides and adhere one button on top of the letter "O" on embossed motif.

Cut an 8½ x 5½-inch piece of pink patterned paper; score and fold in half. Cut a 5¼-inch length from embossed white card stock; cut along one of the wavy lines to form the width of the strip and apply chalk to wavy line. Adhere strip to front of card 1 inch from bottom; fold 1 inch of strip to back of card at left side. Adhere embossed "Love" panel to right side of card with adhesive dots.

For tag, repeat embossing process of the "Love" motif on remaining piece of pink card stock, but omit the outline around perimeter. Cut piece and layer onto white card stock; trim with decorative-edge scissors.

Adhere remaining button on top of the letter "O" and punch a teardrop shape at top of tag. Cut 8 inches of fibers and fold in half; insert fibers through hole forming a loop and pull tails of fibers through loop. Lightly apply chalk on decorative edges of tag. ■

MATERIALS

"Love" brass stencil
Embossing stylus
White wavy-embossed
  card stock
Pink card stock with a
  lighter center core
Pink striped patterned
  paper
Wax paper
2 small white buttons
Single-ply metallic pink
  thread
Sewing needle
White fibers
Pink chalk
Decorative-edge scissors
Teardrop punch
Adhesive dots
Double-sided tape
Removable tape
Bone folder
Sanding block
Ruler
Light box or light source

SOURCES: Papers, stencil and embossing stylus from Lasting Impressions for Paper, Inc.; thread from Kreinik; chalk from Craf-T Products; adhesive dots from Glue Dots.

MATERIALS

Rubber stamps: frog, "Be
    Mine!" and "Happy
    Valentine's Day!"
Card stock: purple, pink
    and light pink
Ink pads: light purple, pink
    and light pink
Small white envelopes to
    fit cards
Metal-edge square tags
Metal-edge round tag
Pink grosgrain ribbon
Hole punch
Adhesive foam squares

Hoppin' Love

Design by R E N A E C U R T Z, *courtesy of Stampin' Up!*

Cut six 5 x 7-inch rectangles from colored card stock; score each and fold in half. Using coordinating inks, stamp frog image onto square tags. Attach a tag to front of each card with adhesive squares. Stamp "Happy Valentine's Day" below each tag.

Use pink ink to stamp "Be Mine!" on round tag; punch hole in tag and thread ribbon through hole. Tie ribbon around stack of cards and envelopes; tie into a knot to secure. ■

SOURCES: Rubber stamps, card stock, ink pads, envelopes, metal-edge tags, ribbon and adhesive foam squares from Stampin' Up!.

Pink Hearts

Design by R E N A E C U R T Z, *courtesy of Stampin' Up!*

MATERIALS

Assorted hearts and
    "valentine" rubber
    stamps
White note cards with
    envelopes
Pink and light pink ink pads
Rose pink grosgrain ribbon
Silver brads
1/16-inch circle punch
Rounded corner punch
Bone folder

Stamp assorted heart images along center of card alternating ink colors; stamp "valentine" below hearts. Punch rounded corner centered toward bottom on back of card. *Note: Rounded shape should face upward.* Punch hole into rounded flap; attach brad to flap. On front of card, fold up a ¼-inch flap; insert flap into rounded slit. Repeat for desired number of cards. Tie ribbon around stack of cards and envelopes. ■

SOURCES: Rubber stamps, note cards, ink pads, brads, ribbon and corner punch from Stampin' Up!.

Keys To My Heart

Design by SANDRA GRAHAM SMITH

CARD

Cut a 5½ x 8½-inch piece of black card stock; score and fold in half. Using die-cut machine, cut one filmstrip shape from red card stock. Cut a 3 x 4½-inch piece of red and white striped paper; glue to back side of filmstrip shape and glue to front of card.

Punch two tag shapes from black card stock; center and glue to openings in filmstrip. Punch two keys from silver card stock; trim as needed. Glue keys at an angle on tags. Punch three hearts from black card stock; glue to filmstrip center with even spacing between each heart.

ENVELOPE

Using die-cut machine, cut one filmstrip shape from red card stock; cut both side strips away from middle section. Cut a piece of red and white striped paper to fit under each filmstrip side; glue striped paper to back of strips. Glue one layered strip to left side of envelope and the other to the back flap.

Punch six hearts from red card stock; glue four to back flap above strip and glue the remaining two to front of envelope referring to photo for placement. Punch three keys from silver card stock; trim edges and glue to front of envelope. ■

SOURCES: Striped paper from Die Cuts with a View; key punches from Punch Bunch; tag punch from EK Success.

MATERIALS

Card stock: black, red and silver

Red and white striped patterned paper

3¾ x 6½-inch black envelope

Die-cut machine

Filmstrip die cut

Punches: small heart, decorative tag and assorted keys

Glue stick

Game of Love

Design by MELANIE BAUER

MATERIALS

- Cream and light pink card stock
- Coordinating patterned paper
- 3 pink buttons
- Assorted alphabet rubber stamps
- Pink ink pad
- Black fine-tip pen
- Glue stick

Cut an 8-inch square from cream card stock; fold in half to form card. Cut a 3-inch square from light pink card stock. Using scraps from the cream card stock, cut and adhere four thin strips to form a tic-tac-toe board on pink square. Cut a 3-inch square from patterned paper; cut in half to form two rectangles that measure 1½ x 3 inches.

Apply pink ink to the edges of the tic-tac-toe square; adhere buttons in center squares of tic-tac-toe board and stamp x's in remaining squares. Referring to photo for placement, adhere patterned paper rectangles to back of tic-tac-toe board and adhere assembled piece to top portion of card.

Stamp the word "love" below game board. Referring to photo, finish card by alternating handwriting with stamping to complete the following sentiment: "in the game of love I consider myself a winner and you are my"; stamp the words "grand prize" inside card. ■

SOURCES: Card stock and paper from Chatterbox; PSX rubber stamps from Duncan; ink pad from Clearsnap.

Romantic Heart

Design by D O N N A C H A P M A N, *courtesy of DMD, Inc.*

Cut two rectangles from patterned card stock, one measuring 3⅝ x 5¼ inches and the other measuring 2 x 3¼ inches. Using foam stencil brush, cover larger rectangle with turquoise ink; cover smaller rectangle with pink ink. Add dark pink to edges. **Note:** *Apply ink so there are light and dark areas of color.* Attach turquoise rectangle to card with glue stick; draw a few random light lines around border with marker. Draw a light border around pink rectangle.

Cut a heart out of white card stock and cover surface with yellow ink; draw a loose line around heart's edge. Attach heart to pink rectangle with adhesive dots; tie a piece of black string around rectangle and heart. Glue pink rectangle to a 2¾ x 4¼-inch piece of white card stock. Referring to photo, draw a wavy line around rectangle; cut along wavy line and attach to center of card with adhesive dots. ∎

SOURCES: Blank card and card stock from DMD, Inc.; ink pads from Tsukineko.

MATERIALS

Blank white card
White card stock
Script writing patterned
  card stock
Ink pads: turquoise, light
  pink, dark pink and
  yellow
Foam stencil brush
Black string
Black fine-tip permanent
  marker
Adhesive foam dots
Glue stick

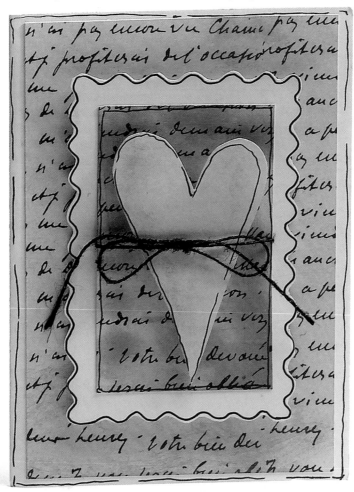

Love Is In The Air

Design courtesy of PM DESIGNS

MATERIALS

Light pink and dark pink card stock

3 pre-colored heart images

Pink fibers

Hole punch

Transparency sheet

Glue stick

Computer font (optional)

Project note: *For adhesive not to show through transparency sheet, apply glue where it will be hidden underneath tags.*

Cut a 5½ x 8½-inch rectangle from dark pink card stock; score and fold in half to form card. Cut a 5 x 3¾-inch rectangle from light pink card stock.

Adhere pre-colored heart images to dark pink card stock and cut area around each into a tag shape. Punch a hole at top of each tag and thread fibers through holes; adhere end to back of light pink rectangle to secure. Adhere light pink rectangle to front of card.

Use a computer to print "Love is in the air ..." onto a transparency sheet; cut a rectangle around words and adhere underneath tags. **Option:** *Use permanent marker to hand-write sentiment.* Adhere tags to card to keep them secure. ■

SOURCES: Pre-colored images from PM Designs; card stock from Paper Adventures; fiber from Fibers By The Yard.

Lovebug

Design by KATIE BOLDT

MATERIALS

Light brown flecked card stock

Coordinating patterned paper

Pre-printed ladybug paper embellishment

Brown fine-tip marker

Glue stick

Cut light brown flecked card stock to 5½ x 8½ inches; score and fold in half. Tear a piece of patterned paper and adhere to upper left corner of card; trim edges. Adhere ladybug embellishment and write "lovebug" underneath embellishment with brown marker. ■

SOURCES: Card stock from Stampin' Up!; patterned paper from Paper Adventures; ladybug embellishment from EK Success.

Heart & Soul

Design by KATIE BOLDT

Cut an 8½ x 5½-inch rectangle from burgundy card stock; score and fold in half. Adhere two love sentiment stickers to front of card at varying angles. Cut a small notched hole in the seam of the card and thread fiber through it; wrap fiber around card and tie a knot toward right side.

Cut a heart shape from textured paper; wrap a piece of craft wire around heart and adhere to tag. Adhere tag to center of card on top of fiber. Attach buttons to bottom left corner of card with adhesive dots and adhere additional word stickers as desired. ∎

SOURCES: Tag from All Nite Scrapper; stickers from Making Memories and Bo-Bunny Press.

MATERIALS

Burgundy card stock
Burgundy textured paper
Tea-stained tag
Thin silver craft wire
Assorted love sentiment
    stickers
Gold fiber
2 brown buttons
Glue stick
Adhesive dots

Vintage Love

Design by STACEY WAKELIN

Cut an 8 x 4-inch piece of light brown card stock; score and fold in half. Cut a 3⅞-inch square from vellum; attach to card using a brad in each corner. Tear a 3 x 2½-inch piece of light brown card stock; apply ink to edges and adhere to center of card. Adhere "L" stencil to torn piece of card stock; stamp the letters "o," "v" and "e" beside the stencil. Apply brown ink randomly over stencil and to edges of card. ∎

SOURCES: Vellum from Karen Foster Design; brads from Making Memories; PSX rubber stamps from Duncan.

MATERIALS

Light brown card stock
Vellum with printed words
4 brown square brads
"L" letter stencil
Alphabet rubber stamps
Brown ink pad
Craft sponge
Glue stick

Happy Easter

Design by LENAE GERIG, *courtesy of Hot Off The Press*

MATERIALS

5 x 6½-inch white card

2 coordinating pink patterned papers

White paper

Pink vellum

Pre-printed pink floral tag

Pink ribbon

Pink fiber

2 mini gold brads

3 gold flower-shaped eyelets

1/16-inch hole punch

Ruler

Computer font (optional)

Draw a small dot at top of card 1½ inches in from fold; draw another dot 1¾ inches down from top edge on fold. Draw a line connecting the dots; cut off line. Repeat for other side.

Trace card front to pink patterned paper; cut pink paper ¼-inch smaller on all sides. Mat pink paper onto white paper leaving a 1/16-inch border. Use a computer or hand-print "Happy Easter" onto pink vellum; let dry and cut a 1-inch-wide strip around words. Secure strip to bottom of layered piece using eyelets and brads.

Adhere different pink patterned paper to front of card; trim edges even. Center and glue layered piece to card; trim vellum edges even. Cut out floral tag; punch a hole at top and set floral eyelet. Fold pink fiber in half and thread through eyelet; thread ends through formed loop and tie a knot. Tie a piece of pink ribbon to fiber and knot both ends. Referring to photo, glue tag to card. ∎

SOURCES: Papers, vellum, tag, ribbon, brads and eyelets from Hot Off The Press.

Easter Bouquet

Design by LENAE GERIG, *courtesy of Hot Off The Press*

Adhere a piece of gray patterned paper to card; trim edges even. Cut a 4½ x 5-inch strip from remaining patterned paper; tear top and bottom edges and adhere to center of card. Cut out embossed letters to spell "EASTER." Apply green chalk to the edges of each letter and to the embossed flower image; glue image to center of card and glue letters below image.

Cut each ribbon into two 6½-inch lengths; hold a green piece and a gray piece together and knot the center. Glue the knot toward the bottom of the card; wrap ends around edges and glue to secure. Repeat for second lengths of ribbon, but place these at top of card. ■

SOURCES: Paper, ribbon, pre-embossed flower image and alphabet squares from Hot Off The Press; chalk from Craf-T Products.

MATERIALS

5 x 6½-inch blank white card

2 coordinating gray patterned papers

13 inches each gray and green ribbon

Pre-embossed flower image

Pre-embossed alphabet squares

Green chalk

Glue stick

Eggstra Special Easter

Design by MARY AYRES

Cut a 5½ x 8½-inch rectangle from light purple card stock; score and fold in half. Tear two ¾-inch-wide strips of blue card stock and one 1¾-inch-wide strip of white card stock; use craft sponge to apply blue ink to torn edges. Glue strips symmetrically across card with white strip in the center; trim ends.

Assemble chick die-cut layers; draw a dashed line around feet, beak and body with light blue marker. Draw eyes with black marker. Referring to photo for placement, adhere eggs and chick to center strip. Use rub-on transfers to apply Easter phrases in upper left and lower right corners. ■

SOURCES: Die cuts from Making Memories; rub-on transfers from Royal & Langnickel; Zip Dry paper adhesive from Beacon.

MATERIALS

Chick and eggs die cuts

Card stock: white, light purple and blue

Easter phrases rub-on transfers

Blue ink pad

Light blue and black fine-tip permanent markers

Craft sponge

Instant-dry paper adhesive

Rotary tool and scoring blade

Party Pig

Design by RENAE CURTZ, *courtesy of Stampin' Up!*

MATERIALS

Party pig and small "x"
   rubber stamps
Card stock: dark pink,
   medium pink, light
   pink, black and white
Black and dark pink ink
   pads
Watercolor brush
Black gingham ribbon
¼-inch circle punch
Adhesive foam squares
Glue stick

Cut a 4¼ x 11-inch piece of dark pink card stock; score and fold in half. Using dark pink ink, stamp "x" image randomly over front of card. Use black ink to stamp pig image onto white card stock; apply color with dark pink ink and watercolor brush. Cut out pig. Layer onto a 1⅞ x 1⁹⁄₁₆-inch piece of light pink card stock and then a 2 x 3-inch piece of black card stock. Tie black gingham ribbon underneath image; punch four circles from varying shades of pink card stock and adhere below ribbon. Attach assembled piece to card using adhesive dots. ■

SOURCES: Rubber stamps, card stock, ink pads, ribbon and adhesive foam squares from Stampin' Up!.

Happy Pig Day

Design by EMILY CALL, *courtesy of Stampin' Up!*

MATERIALS

Pig and "happy day"
   rubber stamps
8½ x 11-inch sage green
   card stock
2¼-inch square cream
   flecked card stock
2½ x 3½-inch blue card
   stock
Blue plaid patterned vellum
Ink pads: black, sage
   green, gray, blue and
   light peach
Watercolor brush
Blue grosgrain ribbon
2 sage green eyelets
Eyelet setter tool
Sewing machine and white
   thread
Glue stick
Adhesive foam squares

Cut an 8½ x 5½-inch piece of sage green card stock; score and fold in half. Using black ink, stamp pig image onto cream flecked card stock; layer square onto a 2⅜-inch square of sage green card stock.

Use watercolor brush and ink pads to apply color to pig image; layer image onto top half of blue card stock. Using blue ink, stamp "happy day" sentiment along bottom edge of blue card stock; tie ribbon above sentiment.

Cut two 2½ x 5½-inch rectangles from vellum; layer rectangles on top of each other and sew them together along fold of card. Set eyelets toward bottom of card; attach layered pig image with foam squares. ■

SOURCES: Rubber stamps, card stock, vellum, ink pads, ribbon and eyelets from Stampin' Up!.

Daisy Greetings

Designs by DEANNA HUTCHISON

Cut a 5 x 8½-inch piece of yellow gingham card stock; score and fold in half. Adhere a 3 x 3¾-inch piece of yellow card stock to a 4¼ x 3½-inch piece of clear vellum. Punch a hole in top two corners of yellow card stock; set eyelets.

Cut a piece of gold wire approximately 3¾ inches; secure one end to back with tape. Thread wire through an eyelet and string on desired beads; insert end through remaining eyelet and secure with a piece of tape. Glue assembled piece to card.

Adhere a 1¼ x 3-inch rectangle cut from the paint chip strip to a 1½ x 3½-inch piece of clear vellum; glue to card. Punch three large daisies from yellow card stock; punch three small daisies from white card stock. Join one small daisy to a large daisy with a gold brad; repeat with remaining daisies to form three flowers. Attach daisies to paint strip with adhesive dots.

For green version, follow basic instructions above but use green gingham card stock instead of yellow gingham, green vellum instead of clear and green beads instead of yellow. ■

MATERIALS

Card stock: green
   gingham, yellow
   gingham, olive green,
   yellow and white
Green and clear vellum
Green and yellow paint
   strips
Green and yellow seed
   beads
Green and amber E beads
3 silver brads
3 gold brads
2 silver eyelets
2 gold eyelets
Silver and gold craft wire
Small and large daisy
   punches
Hole punch
Small adhesive foam dots
Glue stick
Tape

Spring Fling

Design by ALISON BERGQUIST, *courtesy of PM Designs*

MATERIALS

Pre-colored flower images
Card stock: purple, dark
 blue, light blue and
 white
Purple and blue chalk
Silver brads
Alphabet rubber stamps
Black ink pad
Black fine-tip pen
Adhesive foam dots
Glue stick

Cut a 12 x 6-inch rectangle of purple card stock; score and fold in half. Cut a 2½ x 6-inch piece of dark blue card stock and adhere to left side of card. Place silver brads into the corners of three pre-colored flower images; mount images onto light blue card stock and trim around edges leaving approximately a ⅛-inch border. Attach flower images to dark blue card stock strip with adhesive foam dots.

Cut a 2½ x ¾-inch rectangle of white card stock and stamp "SPRING FLING" onto it; apply purple and blue chalk to rectangle and draw an outline around wording with black pen. Mount onto light blue paper; adhere to lower right corner of card and add small dots to rectangle with black pen. ∎

SOURCES: Pre-colored images from PM Designs; chalk from General Pencil Co.; adhesive foam dots from Glue Dots.

Butterfly Fancy

Design by SANDY ROLLINGER

Apply double-sided adhesive sheet to a sheet of blue parchment paper; lay front of card onto parchment paper and trace around perimeter. Cut out paper and adhere to card. Apply adhesive sheet to floral-textured paper; cut around flower areas leaving an uneven edge. Adhere paper to lower left corner of card; trim edges even.

Punch three butterflies from pink parchment paper; punch three butterflies from blue vellum. Attach an adhesive dot on one wing of each butterfly; adhere butterflies randomly on card.

Use white paper paint to make dots on butterflies. Outline textured paper and a few flowers with white paper paint; with blue paper paint, make dots on random areas of textured paper. Let dry completely. ■

SOURCES: Paper paint from Plaid; Zots adhesive dots and PeelnStick adhesive sheets from Therm O Web; textured paper from Provo Craft.

MATERIALS

5 x 7-inch white card with envelope
Floral-textured blue paper
Blue vellum
Blue and pink parchment paper
White and bright blue paper paint
Small butterfly punch
Double-sided adhesive sheets
Adhesive dots

Hollywood Greetings

Design by ANNIE LANG   DIAGRAMS ON PAGE 90

MATERIALS

White stationery paper

Pink patterned paper

White card stock

8 inches ⅛-inch-wide blue
  satin ribbon

3-inch piece pink feathered
  boa

Light blue chalk

Sponge tip applicator

Black fine-tip marker

⅛- and ¾-inch-wide
  double-sided tape

Cut a 2¾ x 7½-inch rectangle from white card stock; cut a rectangle from pink patterned paper the same size. Using double-sided tape, adhere rectangles together; fold rectangle in half with patterned side facing out. Attach ¾-inch-wide double-sided tape along one side of top border on rectangle; adhere the pink feather boa piece to tape.

Open rectangle so white card stock side is facing up; attach a strip of ⅛-inch-wide double-sided tape along side edges. Close the rectangle and press side seams together; trim excess boa piece.

Using pattern provided, trace glove onto white card stock; cut out. On both sides of glove, draw the border and detail lines with fine-tip marker; use sponge tip applicator to apply light blue chalk along edges and detail lines. Fold the thumb section over so it lines up with left side; use a piece of double-sided tape to secure thumb.

Cut a 3½ x 8-inch piece of stationery paper; write message on paper. Roll paper up; tie with satin ribbon and tuck under thumb. Insert glove into sleeve envelope. ■

SOURCES: Double-sided tape and Sticky Dots from Therm O Web.

Mom Celebrated

Design by DEANNA HUTCHISON

Cut a 4¾ x 8-inch piece of pink striped card stock; score and fold in half. Cut a 3½ x 2¾-inch piece of pink paper; crumple up paper. Straighten out paper and lightly sand entire surface. Glue piece to a 3¾ x 3-inch piece of white card stock. Apply pink chalk to four photo corners; adhere photo corners to layered piece.

Cut another small piece of pink paper and crumple up; straighten out and lightly sand surface. Cut a circle from paper to fit onto tag; adhere to tag. Attach adhesive mesh to lower right corner of layered piece; adhere tag on top of mesh using foam tape. Thread fiber through heart charm; adhere charm to tag with an adhesive dot. Wrap fiber ends to back; glue assembled piece to card. Attach letter stickers to upper left corner to spell "MOM." ■

MATERIALS

Pink striped and white
    card stock
Pink paper
Sandpaper
Metal-edge round tag
Adhesive white mesh
Pink fiber
Silver heart charm
4 white photo corners
Metallic pink chalk
Letter stickers
Glue stick
Adhesive foam tape
Adhesive dots

Posies for Mom

Design by KATIE BOLDT

Cut a 5½ x 8½-inch piece of beige card stock; score and fold in half. Cut a 2⅛ x 3-inch rectangle from pink card stock; adhere to front of card. String mini plaque onto fiber; adhere ends of fiber to a 1⅛ x 3½-inch piece of striped paper. Adhere assembled piece across bottom of pink rectangle. Punch three flowers from blue card stock. Referring to photo for placement, adhere flowers to card; set an eyelet in center of each flower. ■

SOURCES: Eyelets from Making Memories; mini plaque from All Nite Scrapper; striped paper from KI Memories.

MATERIALS

Card stock: beige, blue
    and pink
Multi-color striped
    patterned paper
Small flower punch
3 beige eyelets
Pink fiber
"Happy Mother's Day"
    mini plaque with holes
Glue stick

Especially for Mom

Design by SUSAN HUBER

MATERIALS

Golden yellow and purple card stock

Purple vellum tag

2 light purple mini triangle brads

3 light purple mini round brads

Coordinating fibers

Black fine-tip pen

Alphabet stickers

Small square die cut

Adhesive foam tape

Glue stick

Flower photo

Cut an 8½ x 5½-inch piece of golden yellow card stock; score and fold in half. Mat photo on purple card stock leaving a small border; attach to lower left corner of card with adhesive foam tape. Write "especially for" on golden yellow card stock; attach a triangle brad on each side of lettering and cut a rectangle around words. Mat on purple card stock leaving a small border; attach above flower photo with adhesive foam tape.

Cut three small squares from golden yellow card stock using die cut; adhere to vellum tag. Place alphabet stickers on squares spelling "MOM." Insert a mini round brad into the top of each square. Fold several fibers together in half; thread fibers through hole in tag and insert ends through formed loop. Layer tag on purple card stock with adhesive foam tape; adhere assembled tag to empty area of card. ■

SOURCES: Vellum tag from American Tag; brads from Lasting Impressions for Paper Inc.; alphabet stickers from Memories Complete.

Sweet Baby

Design by DEANNA HUTCHISON

Cut an 8½ x 5½-inch piece of blue card stock; score and fold in half. Cut a 4 x 5¼-inch piece of light blue card stock; adhere to card. Cut a 1½ x 4-inch strip of blue card stock and adhere toward top section of card. Cut a 1¼ x 4-inch strip of light blue card stock; layer on top of blue strip.

Adhere a 2½-inch square of light blue card stock to a 2¾-inch square of blue card stock; set a brad in each corner of light blue square. Attach teddy bear sticker to a 2-inch square of dark blue card stock; attach to layered square with foam tape. Adhere assembled square over top strip on card.

Place "Sweet Baby" sticker toward bottom of card; wrap fibers around fold of card and tie a knot inside. ∎

SOURCES: Stickers from Pebbles Inc.

MATERIALS

Blue and light blue card
    stock
Black and white teddy
    bear sticker
"Sweet Baby" label sticker
Blue fibers
4 silver brads
Adhesive foam tape
Glue stick

Baby Pin

Design by DEANNA HUTCHISON

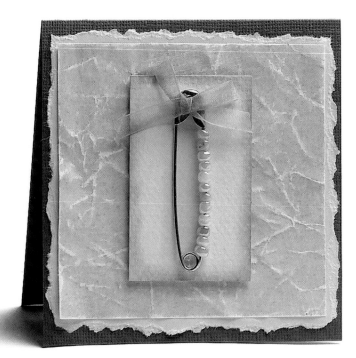

Cut a 3¾ x 7¾-inch piece of dark purple card stock; score and fold in half. Tear a 3¾-inch square from white card stock; adhere to card. Cut a 3¼-inch square from light purple paper and crumple up; straighten out paper and lightly sand entire surface. Adhere to card.

Cut a 1½ x 2½-inch rectangle from white card stock; apply purple chalk to edges. Attach to card with adhesive foam tape. Thread beads onto safety pin; attach pin to card with adhesive dots. Tie a piece of ribbon into a bow; attach to top of pin with an adhesive dot. ∎

MATERIALS

Dark purple and white
    card stock
Light purple paper
Large safety pin
Coordinating pastel beads
Sheer purple ribbon
Purple chalk
Sandpaper
Adhesive foam tape
Adhesive dots
Glue stick

Precious Footprints

Design by BARBARA MATTHIESSEN

MATERIALS

- 6 x 8-inch light blue card stock
- 3¼ x 5¼-inch white card stock
- Baby feet casting mold
- 6 cotton linter casting squares
- White webbing spray
- Children sentiment rubber stamp
- Bright blue ink pad
- Dime-size piece deep blue tissue paper
- Paper adhesive
- Blender
- Kitchen strainer
- Sponge
- Paper towels

Following manufacturer's instructions, apply a layer of webbing spray to both sides of light blue card stock; let dry. **Note:** *Allow first side to dry before proceeding to other side.*

Follow instructions on cotton linter square package adding a small piece of deep blue tissue paper at end of blending process. Cast paper mold following package instructions; let dry.

Fold sprayed blue card stock in half; stamp children sentiment on bottom edge of white card stock. Adhere stamped card stock and cast paper to card. ■

SOURCES: Casting mold and cotton linter casting squares from Arnold Grummer's; webbing spray from Krylon; rubber stamp from Uptown Design Co.

I love little children, and it is not a slight thing when they, who are fresh from God, love us.
~ Charles Dickens

Playful Pocket Cards

Design by LISA ROJAS

Stamp desired girl or boy rubber stamp images twice onto white card stock. Use sponge-tip applicators and chalk pastels to add color to each image; apply a layer of spray sealer to each and allow to dry completely.

Cut out images; adhere foam squares to one set of the stamped images and attach them to the other set of images, giving a dimensional effect. Apply pink or white ribbon along the edges of the diaper with hot-glue gun to cover foam squares.

Fold light purple or light blue card stock in half; adhere pink or light blue checkered paper with double-stick tape. Referring to photo for placement, adhere diaper and baby girl or boy bear images to card with craft glue; fill opening of diaper with white or yellow raffia.

Apply glue to the end of a toothpick; adhere to one of the stamped images. Repeat process for all stamped images. Apply glue to opposite ends of toothpicks; stick each toothpick into diaper.

Stamp baby sentiment image onto white card stock; cut out with decorative-edge scissors. Mount onto light purple or red card stock; cut out with decorative-edge scissors. Glue light purple or red chenille stem to back of sentiment; insert into diaper. For girl card, glue mini baby rattles to front bottom corners. ■

SOURCES: Spray sealer from Krylon; rubber stamps from Darcie's Country Folk.

MATERIALS

- 5½ x 8½-inch pieces light purple and light blue card stock
- 2 (8½ x 11-inch) white card stock
- 3¼ x 2-inch red card stock
- 5¼ x 4-inch pieces pink checkered and light blue checkered paper
- Rubber stamps: large baby diaper, baby girl bear, baby boy bear, rattle, spinning toy, baby blocks, toy ducky, soccer ball, basketball, football, toy train, ball and glove and baby sentiment
- Black permanent ink pad
- Chalk pastels
- Small sponge-tip applicators
- Spray sealer
- Mini baby rattles
- White and yellow crinkled paper raffia
- Light purple and red chenille stems
- ¼-inch-wide pink and white ribbon
- Decorative-edge scissors
- Adhesive foam squares
- Craft glue
- Hot-glue gun
- Toothpicks
- Double-stick tape

Dearest Father

Design by M A R Y A Y R E S

Cut an 8 x 10-inch rectangle from medium brown card stock; score and fold in half. Cut an 8 x 4½-inch rectangle from dark brown card stock; tear along the long edges. Using craft sponge, apply black ink to torn edges and adhere to card.

Cut an 8 x 3-inch rectangle from patterned scrapbook paper; tear along long edges. Apply brown ink to torn edges and adhere toward right side of card.

Cut a 2¾ x 4-inch rectangle from vellum; tear top edge. Apply brown ink to edges. Punch a ⅛-inch hole in upper right corner of rectangle; attach antique brass eyelet.

Transfer father sentiment to off-white card stock; cut a ⅝ x 3⅜-inch rectangle around words leaving extra space on right side for eyelet. Apply brown ink to edges; punch a ⅛-inch hole in rectangle and attach antique brass eyelet.

Insert hemp cord through eyelets in rectangle and vellum; knot ends together and trim ends. Place vellum rectangle toward bottom of card; machine-stitch around sides and bottom ⅛ inch from edges to form a pocket. Apply paper adhesive to back of word rectangle to secure.

For tag, cut a 2½ x 6-inch rectangle from light brown card stock; cut top corners diagonally and apply brown ink to edges. Attach black corners to photo and adhere photo to tag. Punch a ³⁄₁₆-inch hole at top of tag; attach decorative eyelet.

Cut 8-inch lengths of gray fibers; fold in half and insert ends through eyelet from back to front. Bring ends back through formed loop; trim ends 2 inches from tag and place tag in vellum pocket. Apply a small amount of paper adhesive to back of tag to secure. ■

SOURCES: Patterned paper from K&Company; rub-on transfer from Royal & Langnickel; eyelet from Creative Imaginations; Zip Dry paper adhesive from Beacon.

MATERIALS

- Card stock: off-white, light brown, medium brown and dark brown
- Document patterned paper
- Ivory vellum
- Father sentiment rub-on transfer
- Gray fibers
- Hemp cord
- ³⁄₁₆-inch decorative eyelet
- 2 (⅛-inch) round antique brass eyelets
- Black sewing thread
- Sewing machine
- 4 black photo corners
- Brown and black ink pads
- Craft sponge
- Instant-dry paper adhesive
- ⅛- and ³⁄₁₆-inch circle punches
- 2¼ x 5-inch photo

Happy Father's Day

Design by DEANNA HUTCHISON

MATERIALS

Brown and olive green card stock

Coordinating patterned paper

4 olive green brads

Metallic gold ink pad

Craft sponge

Paper crimper

Adhesive foam tape

Computer font (optional)

Cut a 5½ x 8¼-inch piece of brown card stock; score and fold in half. Adhere a 1⅞ x 3½-inch piece of patterned paper toward the left side of a 5¼ x 4-inch piece of olive green card stock; attach an eyelet in each corner of patterned rectangle. Adhere assembled piece to card.

Cut a 3¾ x 2-inch piece of brown card stock; run through paper crimper and apply metallic gold ink to raised areas. Use a computer or hand-print "Happy Father's Day!" on olive green card stock; cut a rectangle around words and tear bottom edge. Adhere to crimped card stock; attach assembled piece to card using adhesive foam tape. ∎

A Father Is …

Design by LORINE MASON

MATERIALS

Father sentiment quotes

Ivory and light brown card stock

¼-inch-wide paper quilling strips in natural colors

Light brown ink pad

Adhesive foam squares

Glue stick

Paper trimmer

Cut an 8½ x 8-inch piece of ivory card stock; score and fold in half. Cut two pieces of light brown card stock, one measuring 3 x 5⅛ inches and the other measuring 3 x 4¾ inches. Use a glue stick to randomly apply quilling strips across front of folded card; apply additional quilling strips to the first light brown piece. Center and glue the embellished light brown piece to front of card.

Cut out desired quote; apply light brown ink to edges and let dry. Use adhesive squares to attach to card.

Cut a second quote; adhere to second light brown piece. Glue a quilling strip angled inside card; center and glue second quote over strip. ∎

SOURCES: Sentiment quotes from Hot Off The Press.

A Tribute To Dad

Design by NANCY BILLETDEAUX

Fold white card stock in half; set aside. Cut an 8½ x 11-inch piece of document patterned paper. Cut out "D," "A" and "D" from tag letters; attach to lower left corner of patterned paper with an eyelet at the top of each tag. Adhere patterned paper to card stock.

Referring to photo for placement, place adhesive mesh on card; place word stickers on top of mesh. Punch out three keys from bronze metal and glue to card. Insert metallic fiber inside fold of card and thread it through to center top of card; tie into a knot.

To embellish envelope, place envelope flap onto patterned paper and trace around flap; cut out and adhere. ■

SOURCES: Patterned paper from Karen Foster Design; stickers, fiber and sheet metal from EK Success; key punches from Punch Bunch; adhesive mesh from Magic Mesh; tag letters from Hot Off The Press.

MATERIALS

- 8½ x 11-inch white card stock
- 5¾ x 8¾-inch white envelope
- 12 x 12-inch document patterned paper
- Clear adhesive word stickers: courage, honor and bravery
- 3 assorted key punches
- 2 x 2½-inch adhesive copper mesh
- Tag letters
- Bronze sheet metal
- 24 inches metallic beige fiber
- 3 (⅛-inch) bronze eyelets
- Eyelet setter
- Glue

Engagement Congrats

Design by KATIE BOLDT

MATERIALS

Gray-blue card stock
Script writing patterned
     paper
Metal-edge vellum circle
     tag
Black and white fiber
Wedding and letter stickers
Black fine-tip marker
Silver gel pen
Double-sided tape
Glue stick

Cut a 5½ x 8½-inch piece of gray-blue card stock; score and fold in half. Tear a piece of patterned paper; adhere to upper left corner of card and trim edges even. Place wedding stickers in desired positions on vellum tag; insert fiber through hole in tag and tie. Adhere to center of card. Use letter stickers to spell "congrats" below tag. Use the black marker to write "on your engagement!" underneath letter stickers; outline sentiment with silver gel pen. ■

SOURCES: Vellum tag from Making Memories; stickers from Treehouse Designs and SEI.

Celebrate Your Day

Design Courtesy of Duncan

MATERIALS

Vellum square card
Pink patterned paper
3¼ x 4-inch white
     iridescent paper
Wedding attire die cuts
Wedding sentiment rub-on
     transfer
1 yard ⅜-inch-wide pink
     organza ribbon
Light pink dimensional
     paper paint
Mounting squares
Adhesive foam squares
Decorative-edge scissors
Paper towel

Cut a piece of pink patterned paper the same size as vellum card; fold and insert into card. Thread ribbon through card and tie into a bow at center top. Trim edges of iridescent paper with decorative-edge scissors; position and attach die cuts onto paper using adhesive squares. Create stitch marks around edge of piece with dimensional paper paint; let dry. ***Note:*** *Make sure to begin flow of paint on paper towel before moving to card.* Attach iridescent piece to card with mounting squares.

Tear 1 inch of vellum from bottom front of card; transfer sentiment to bottom of pink patterned paper. ■

SOURCES: PSX iridescent paper, patterned paper, mounting squares, dimensional paper paint, rub-on transfer, die cuts and vellum card from Duncan.

On Your Wedding Day

Design by LEE MCKENNEY

Cut a 5 x 7-inch piece of iridescent cream paper. Use a computer font or hand-print desired words centered on bottom of paper. Adhere to card with double-sided tape.

Cut a 4¼ x 5½-inch piece of wedding sentiments patterned paper; cut a piece of vellum the same size. Layer the vellum over the patterned paper and place a piece of double-sided tape in the lower right corner to secure. Punch a hole in the top corners of layered piece; insert flower brads to join together.

Cut a 4¼ x 5½-inch piece of textured paper; cut it in half to create a triangle. Layer triangle on bottom right corner of vellum; adhere with glue. ***Note:*** *Lay several books on top of textured paper until glue has dried.*

Once dry, attach layered piece to card; adhere pre-embellished tag angled on front of card. Punch two flowers from textured paper; adhere a flat-back pearl to center of each flower and let dry. Referring to photo, adhere flowers to card. ■

SOURCES: Iridescent paper from Hot Off The Press; textured paper from Ellison; brads from Making Memories; pre-embellished tag from EK Success.

MATERIALS

- 5 x 7-inch cream card
- Iridescent cream paper
- Textured iridescent cream paper
- Wedding sentiments patterned paper
- Clear vellum
- Pre-embellished wedding tag
- 2 flat-back pearls
- Medium flower punch
- 2 mini brass flower brads
- ⅛-inch hole punch
- Craft glue
- Double-sided tape
- Computer font (optional)

MATERIALS

- 4¼ x 5½-inch white heavyweight card stock
- 4¼ x 5½-inch clear vellum
- Wedding cake rubber stamp
- Black waterproof ink
- Watercolor markers
- Heart border template
- Embossing stylus
- ¼-inch-wide organdy ribbon
- ¹⁄₁₆-inch rectangle punch
- Removable tape
- Light box or light source

Sweet Wedding Wishes

Design by LAURIE D'AMBROSIO

Fold vellum and card stock in half. Stamp cake image to center of card stock; color with markers. Unfold vellum; position and tape heart border template right side up to front half of vellum. Turn template over and place onto a light source. Use stylus to emboss design; layer embossed vellum onto card stock with embossed border framing cake image. Punch two rectangles close to the fold through both layers; thread ribbon through holes and tie into a bow. ∎

SOURCES: Watercolor markers from Tombow; template from Fiskars; rubber stamp from Inkadinkado.

Wedding Elegance DIAGRAMS ON PAGE 90

Design by BARB CHAUNCEY

MATERIALS

- Heavyweight vellum
- 10³⁄₈ x 6³⁄₈-inch white card stock
- Tracing paper
- ⅛-inch-wide white iridescent iron-on ribbon
- Mini iron
- Colored chalks
- Double-sided tape
- Craft knife
- Computer font (optional)

Transfer provided pattern to tracing paper. Tape edges of vellum to traced pattern. Following manufacturer's instructions, use a mini iron to apply ribbon to pattern lines. *Note: Apply centers of flowers first so the ends of the ribbon can be covered with the outline of the flower.*

Once all ribbon has been applied, carefully remove vellum from pattern and apply chalk to the back of the vellum behind leaves and flowers. Use craft knife to remove center of heart cutting close to ribbon.

Score and fold white card stock in half to determine placement of front and inside sentiments; unfold card stock and use a computer font or hand-print desired front and inside sentiments. Trim vellum heart to fit front of card; attach vellum to card using double-sided tape at corners. ∎

SOURCES: Iron-on ribbon from Kreinik.

Wed this day
before the Lord,
with loved ones and friends;
Together now, forever more
God bless this family:

Kevin Doyle
&
Marie Louise Adams

With This Ring DIAGRAMS ON PAGE 91

Design by BROOKE SMITH

Project Notes: *Protective gloves are recommended when working with metal to protect against sharp edges. Sand rough edges of metal after cutting.*

Cut cream card stock 11 x 5½ inches; score and fold in half. With craft knife, cut a 2-inch-square opening in upper right corner ½ inch from both edges. Cut an 11 x 1½-inch strip of gray card stock. Place over front of card with right side extending 1½ inches; fold strip around card and secure portion on card front with glue. Glue a 2 x 1-inch piece of cream card stock to right side of short end of gray strip for closure tab. Cut a 1-inch vertical slit in opposite end of gray strip and insert tab to close, then glue a ¾-inch square of gray card stock on end of cream tab that is exposed after closing. With silver paint pen, write "With this ring ..." across gray strip on front of card.

Cut a 1⅝-inch square from cream card stock; glue onto a 1⅞-inch square of gray card stock. Cut two 1-inch circles from crafting metal; cut a ½-inch circle from center of each to make rings. Glue rings in center of cream square. Close card and use adhesive foam squares to attach card-stock square with rings inside front opening. Open card; using pattern provided, cut inside mat from gray card stock and glue inside card. ■

MATERIALS

Cream and gray card stock
Extra-fine-point silver paint
    pen
Silver crafting metal
Tin snips
Craft knife
Sandpaper
Adhesive foam squares
Glue stick
Craft glue
Protective work gloves

Just Married

Design by HEATHER D. WHITE

Cut patterned card stock 5½ x 8½ inches; score and fold in half. Adhere a 5½ x 4¼-inch piece of patterned card stock on card front; trim edges even. Cut a 5½ x 3-inch piece of patterned card stock; tear top and bottom edges. Glue to center of card lining up side edges. Cut out two wedding images; mat on patterned card stock leaving a small border. Adhere images to card. ■

SOURCES: Card stock and wedding images from Pebbles Inc.

MATERIALS

Black and white words
    patterned card stock
Black and white wedding
    images
Glue stick
Bone folder

Victorian Bouquet

Design by JULIE EBERSOLE

MATERIALS

Pale pink card stock

Sage green patterned
   paper

2 matching flower die cuts

Pre-printed "Happy
   Anniversary" tag

¼-inch adhesive foam dots

Cut a 5½ x 8½-inch piece of pale pink card stock; score and fold in half. Cut a 4 x 5¼-inch piece of patterned paper; adhere to card. Mount flower die cut with glue stick; to add dimension, use adhesive dots to mount desired areas of matching flower die cut. Adhere tag sentiment beside flower image. ■

SOURCES: Patterned paper, die cuts and tag from Anna Griffin Inc.

Silver Anniversary

Design by J U L I E   J A N S E N

Cut an 8½ x 5½-inch piece of white card stock; score and fold in half. Cut a 4 x 5¼-inch piece of silver vellum; adhere to card. Cut two pieces from textured white card stock that both measure 3¾ x 1 inches. Cut one 2½-inch square and one 1 x 2½-inch piece, both from textured white card stock. Referring to photo for placement, adhere strips to card. Stamp "Happy Anniversary" sentiment across bottom strip; attach embellished stickers to remaining strips. If desired, stamp an anniversary sentiment inside card. ■

SOURCES: Card stock from Bazzill Basics; vellum from Hot Off The Press; stickers from EK Success.

MATERIALS

White card stock

Textured white card stock

Metallic silver vellum

25th anniversary embellished stickers

Gray ink pad

"Happy Anniversary" rubber stamp

Glue stick

Anniversary sentiment rubber stamp (optional)

Golden Anniversary

Design by J U L I E   J A N S E N

Cut an 8½ x 5½-inch piece of white card stock; score and fold in half. Cut a 4 x 5¼-inch piece of gold card stock; adhere to card. Cut three strips from textured peach card stock in the following measurements: 1 x 3⅝ inches, 3¾ x 1¼ inches and 2⅝ x 3⅝ inches. Referring to photo for placement, adhere strips to card. Stamp "Happy Anniversary" sentiment across bottom strip; attach embellished stickers to remaining strips. If desired, stamp an anniversary sentiment inside card. ■

SOURCES: Card stock from Bazzill Basics and Hot Off The Press; stickers from EK Success.

MATERIALS

White card stock

Textured peach card stock

Metallic gold card stock

50th anniversary embellished stickers

Black ink pad

"Happy Anniversary" rubber stamp

Glue stick

Anniversary sentiment rubber stamp (optional)

Happy Birthday America

Design by D O X I E   K E L L E R   DIAGRAMS ON PAGE 92

MATERIALS

- Heavyweight white card with envelope
- Watercolor pencils
- Matte-finish spray sealer
- Gray graphite paper
- Black permanent pen
- Round and shader paintbrushes
- White eraser
- Pencil sharpener
- Stylus

Trace pattern to front of card using graphite paper and a stylus. Add color as directed. ***Note:*** *To fill in areas, first use dry watercolor pencils and then apply water to activate color.*

Heart: Paint dark pink; shade with blue.

Sunflower: Paint petals yellow; shade with dark orange. Paint center green; shade with dark pink. Paint leaf light green; shade dark green. Once dry, add seeds to center with black pen.

Watermelon: Paint center dark pink; shade with blue. Paint rind light green and shade with green. Once dry, add seeds with black pen.

Flag: Paint four alternating stripes dark pink; shade with blue. Paint square section blue; paint pole yellow.

Small flowers: Paint petals yellow; shade with orange and dark green. Paint leaves green.

Add lettering and wavy border with black pen. Allow card to dry for several hours. Erase all tracing lines with a white eraser; outline all design elements with black pen. Spray a light layer of matte-finish sealer.

ENVELOPE

Transfer smaller pattern to top left corner of envelope in same manner as card. Add a flower to bottom corners. Apply color in same manner as card.

Heart: Paint dark pink; shade with blue.

Flowers: Paint yellow; shade with dark pink and orange.

Leaves: Paint light green. ■

SOURCES: Card and envelope from Martin F. Weber; paintbrushes and watercolor pencils from Loew-Cornell; matte-finish spray sealer from DecoArt.

Stars & Stripes

Design by B A R B A R A   G R E V E

Place rice paper on felt and use spray bottle of water to moisten paper. Using 1-inch foam brush for each color, paint alternating blue, red and white stripes across paper, immediately spraying each strip with water to mingle colors. Stamp white stars randomly over stripes and spray with water. Carefully remove paper from felt and let dry. Replace paper on felt and moisten again; stamp silver metallic stars randomly over paper. Let dry again.

Fold card stock in half to make a 5 x 7-inch card. Cut a 4 x 4½-inch piece and a 4 x 1½-inch piece from rice paper; position on card front and lightly mark with pencil. Apply glue stick to marked areas, then place papers onto glued areas and press down, smoothing out wrinkles from the center outward. Weight under heavy object until dry. Embellish with fibers and beads. ■

SOURCES: Acrylic paint from DecoArt; fibers from EK Success.

MATERIALS

- 8½ x 11-inch white rice paper
- 10 x 7-inch red card stock
- Acrylic paint: red, white, blue and silver metallic
- 3 (1-inch) foam brushes
- 2-inch star-shaped foam stamp
- Spray bottle of water
- 9 x 12-inch white felt
- Assorted fibers and beads
- Glue stick

Summer Sailing DIAGRAMS ON PAGE 93

Design by MARY AYRES

MATERIALS

Card stock: red, white and blue
Red-and-white check paper
Blue waves patterned paper
Metal word tag
5¼ inches ⅛-inch wooden dowel
5 inches ¼-inch-wide red satin ribbon
Blue craft thread
Sewing machine with white all-purpose thread
4 round silver eyelets and setter tool
⅛-inch circle punch
Decorative-edge scissors
Rotary tool and scoring blade (optional)
¼-inch adhesive foam squares
1-inch star punch
Permanent fabric adhesive

Cut a 10 x 7-inch piece of white card stock; score and fold in half. Glue a 6¾ x 4¾-inch rectangle from blue waves patterned paper to card. Cut sails and boat from card stock as indicated on pattern; glue to card. Punch a star from red-and-white check paper; mat onto blue card stock and glue to right-hand sail. Machine-stitch around inside edges of sails and outside edges of star. Punch holes and set eyelets at points indicated on patterns. Glue wooden dowel between sails, leaving top 1 inch of dowel free.

Insert blue craft thread through eyelets, crossing over dowel at top and bottom; knot ends on back. Thread ribbon through metal tag; glue tag to card and tie ribbon ends loosely around top of dowel. Trim ribbon ends in V-notches and glue to card.

Cut a 4½ x ¾-inch rectangle from blue card stock; trim long edges with decorative-edge scissors to simulate waves. Use adhesive foam squares to attach waves to bottom of card. ∎

SOURCES: Red-and-white check paper from The Paper Patch; blue wave patterned paper from Flavia Weedn Family Trust; metal tag from K&Company; adhesive from Beacon.

Beaded Thanks

Design by KATIE BOLDT

Cut pale peach card stock 5½ x 8½ inches; score and fold in half. Place flower or fern sticker on wood chip; cover surface of wood chip with double-stick beading tape and apply micro beads. Position and stamp "thanks" on card front; adhere beaded wood chip above sentiment with rubber cement. ■

SOURCES: Stickers from Mrs. Grossman's.

MATERIALS
Pale peach card stock
Small wood chip
Flower *or* fern sticker
Clear micro beads
"Thanks" rubber stamp
Black ink pad
Double-stick beading tape
Rubber cement

Thank You Bookmark

Design by ELEEN HULL

MATERIALS

Golden yellow card stock

Clear vellum

Pressed flower

"Thank You" sentiment stamp

Brown ink pad

4 gold brads

1⅜-inch square punch

Craft glue

Cut golden yellow card stock 2 x 8 inches; punch out a square at top. Fold top 2 inches over toward front to create a flap. Stamp "Thank You" sentiment inside square opening. Glue pressed flower to bookmark. Cut vellum 1¾ x 3½ inches; lay vellum over flower and attach to bookmark with brads. ∎

SOURCES: Rubber stamp from Hero Arts.

You Are Great

Design by ELEEN HULL

MATERIALS

Brown flecked card stock

Clear vellum

Green patterned paper

Library pocket and card

Rubber stamps: alphabet set, "friends" circle and "thanks" definition

Ink pads: brown, green and black

2 mini copper eyelets

Jute

Small pressed fern

Silver heart charm

Glue stick

Double-sided tape

Cut brown card stock 6¼ x 9¼ inches; score and fold in half. Use brown ink to randomly stamp "thanks" and "friends" images onto card. Stamp a personalized message on library pocket and card with alphabet stamps and black ink. Gently crumple library card; smooth it out and lightly apply brown ink to random areas.

Stamp "thanks" image onto vellum with green ink; tear around edges and apply brown ink to torn areas. Mount vellum onto a piece of green patterned paper cut slightly larger than vellum.

Glue pressed fern to front of card angled toward the left. Position library card and pocket at an angle on front of card; mark placement of eyelets. Set eyelets.

Use double-sided tape to attach layered vellum piece to the front of the library pocket. Fold bottom underneath pocket and attach pocket to card. Thread jute through eyelets and wrap around pocket; add heart charm and tie into a knot. Trim ends if necessary. ∎

SOURCES: Rubber stamps from Hero Arts.

Gratitude

Design by SHAUNA BERGLUND-IMMEL,
courtesy of Hot Off The Press

Trim ½ inch from bottom edge of card front. Cut a piece of purple patterned paper to fit the inside of card; adhere inside and apply black ink to edges with a craft sponge. Choose a different patterned paper; cut a piece to fit front of card and adhere. Apply black ink to edges.

Cut out desired word labels and glue inside card, lining up tops of labels with the bottom edge of front so they show even when card is closed. Cut out desired sentiment quote; apply black ink to edges. Use a craft knife to cut out the center part of sentiment; emboss with clear embossing powder. Mount onto purple patterned paper and trim edges. Apply black ink to edges. Layer the cut sentiment quote onto purple patterned paper; apply black ink to edges. Referring to photo, attach sentiment to card with adhesive foam tape.

Cut out additional word labels and attach heart clips to labels; adhere to card. Punch three holes at top right corner of card; thread ribbon through each hole and tie into a knot. ∎

Sources: Patterned papers, sentiment quotes and labels, ribbon and heart clips from Hot Off The Press; ink pads from Tsukineko.

MATERIALS

5 x 6½-inch white card

3 assorted purple patterned papers

Gratitude sentiment quotes

Gratitude sentiment word labels

Light purple ribbon

2 silver heart clips

Purple fine-tip pen

Black and watermark ink pads

Clear embossing powder

Embossing heat tool

Hole punch

Craft sponge

Craft knife

Glue stick

Adhesive foam tape

You Inspire Me

Design by PARIS DUKES, *courtesy of Hot Off The Press*

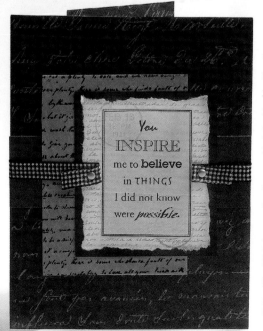

Adhere black text patterned paper to card; trim edges even. Tear edges around desired friendship quote and mat onto iridescent paper. Stamp text image onto a 3 x 4⅛-inch vellum rectangle; let dry and adhere layered friendship quote to right side of vellum. Referring to photo, add a piece of ribbon to each side, folding the ribbon and attaching with a brad.

Cut a 1½-inch-wide strip of red patterned paper; center and adhere assembled quote to strip gluing ribbon ends behind it. Center and adhere to front of card.

For the inside of card, glue a strip of the black patterned paper vertically. Mat the remaining quote to iridescent paper; mat again onto red patterned paper and glue to inside center of card. ∎

Sources: Patterned papers, vellum, ribbon and brads from Hot Off The Press; rubber stamp from Inkadinkado.

MATERIALS

5 x 6½-inch white card

Black text and red patterned papers

Black iridescent paper

Clear vellum

2 friendship quotes

Black gingham ribbon

2 mini antique pewter brads

Text image rubber stamp

Black ink pad

Small hole punch

Glue stick

Craft glue

A Simple Thanks

Design by KATIE BOLDT

MATERIALS

Light blue card stock

Purple wavy corrugated
paper

Metal-edge round purple
tag

Butterfly sticker

Letter stickers

Glue stick

Cut light blue card stock 5½ x 8½ inches; score and fold in half. Cut a 2-inch-wide strip of purple corrugated paper; adhere to left side and trim edges even with card. Attach butterfly sticker to tag; center and adhere tag to card. Position letter stickers on lower right corner to spell "thanks." ◼

Sources: Metal-edge tag from Making Memories; letter stickers from SEI.

Thanks

Design by HEATHER D. WHITE

MATERIALS

White card stock

Lime green patterned
paper

Coordinating striped
paper

Metal-edge round vellum
tag

Coordinating "thanks"
circle tag

5 silver brads

White string

Glue stick

Adhesive dots

Cut white card stock 5½ x 8½ inches; score and fold in half. Cut lime green patterned paper 5½ x 4¼ inches; cut striped paper 2¾ x 4¼ inches and adhere to left side of lime green paper lining up edges. Attach five brads along right edge of striped paper. Insert string through round vellum tag; adhere "thanks" tag to vellum tag. Secure vellum tag to lower right corner of layered papers with an adhesive dot; wrap string ends around back of paper. Adhere assembled piece to front of card; if necessary, trim edges even. ◼

Sources: Patterned papers and circle tag from KI Memories; vellum tag from Making Memories.

Voyage

Design by PARIS DUKES, *courtesy of Hot Off The Press*

Adhere compass patterned paper to front of card; trim edges even with card. Cut out "voyage" definition image leaving extra room on left side. Mat on black card stock; mat again on metallic gold paper. Attach three gold brads on left side; attach layered rectangle to card with foam tape. Tie gold fibers into a knot around each brad; trim ends. Cut out three desired word embellishments and adhere to fibers with foam tape.

For the inside of card, center and adhere a 3¾ x 5½-inch rectangle from compass patterned paper. Add message with desired word embellishments. ∎

MATERIALS

5 x 6½-inch white card
Black card stock
Metallic gold paper
Compass patterned paper
"Voyage" definition image
Gold fibers
Pre-embossed gold word embellishments
Gold brads
Adhesive foam tape
Glue stick

SOURCES: Papers, card stock, definition image, fibers and word embellishments from Hot Off The Press.

For the Journey

Design by LEE MCKENNEY

Cut yellow card stock 8½ x 5½ inches; score and fold in half. Stamp "Paris" image randomly on front of card. Cut two Paris images each approximately 1¾ x 2 inches. Use double-sided tape to adhere images to the backside of filmstrip die cut; trim any edges that show through side holes. Thread fiber through holes; secure ends in back. Adhere filmstrip to card; adhere metal word tag to center of strip. ∎

SOURCES: Rubber stamp from Inkadinkado; die cut from Ellison; tag from Hot Off The Press.

MATERIALS

Yellow and black card stock
"Paris" rubber stamp
Black inkpad
Filmstrip die cut
Multi-colored fiber
Metal "Journey" word tag
Paris images
Double-sided tape

Birthday Celebration

MATERIALS

Purple card stock
Clear vellum
Pre-colored party hat block
Alphabet blocks
Green paint strip
Purple chalk pencil
Orange raffia
Turquoise tinsel strands
Round green brad
Black fine-tip pen
Adhesive foam dots
Glue stick

Design by A L I S O N   B E R G Q U I S T,
courtesy of PM Designs

Cut purple card stock 5½ x 8½ inches; score and fold in half. Center and adhere paint strip horizontally on card; trim edges even. Cut out letters to spell "happy" from alphabet blocks; add color to each with purple chalk pencil and adhere on top portion of card. Tear a piece of vellum; write "birthday" on it and attach to card with green brad. Tie raffia around bottom of card. Place strands of tinsel on remaining area of card; using adhesive foam dots, mount pre-colored party hat image on top of tinsel strands. ∎

SOURCES: Pre-colored block, paint strip and alphabet blocks from PM Designs; chalk pencils from General Pencil Co.

Pocketful of Greetings

MATERIALS

Denim pocket and "happy birthday" rubber stamps
Navy blue, brown, red and white card stock
Blue and white ink pads
2 copper eyelets
Sanding block
Glue stick

Design by J U L I E   E B E R S O L E

Cut brown card stock 5½ x 8½ inches; score and fold in half. Cut a 3⅞ x 5⅛-inch rectangle from navy blue card stock; sand entire surface with sanding block. Stamp birthday sentiment along entire perimeter of rectangle with white ink. Use blue ink to stamp denim pocket image onto white card stock; cut image out. Trim a small rectangle from red card stock; adhere to reverse side of pocket to simulate "tag" sticking out from side of pocket. Apply adhesive along edges of pocket only and mount to navy rectangle. Attach copper eyelets at top corners of pocket; mount navy rectangle to card. ∎

SOURCES: Rubber stamps from JudiKins and A Muse Art Stamps.

Birthday Wishes

Design by DEANNA HUTCHISON

Cut dark green card stock 5½ x 8 inches; score and fold in half. Cut green patterned paper 5½ x 4 inches; tear all edges. Cut a 2 x 4-inch rectangle from dark green card stock; run through paper crimper. Center and adhere at an angle on torn rectangle.

Use a computer or hand-print "Happy Birthday!" on green flecked paper; tear a rectangle around words. Attach square brad to lower right corner and adhere to crimped rectangle.

Wrap ribbon crisscrossed around the left side of layered rectangle; attach spiral clip to center of ribbons with an adhesive dot. Adhere assembled piece to card. ∎

MATERIALS

Dark green card stock
Green patterned paper
Green flecked paper
Sheer white ribbon
Small silver square brad
Silver spiral clip
Paper crimper
Adhesive dots
Computer font (optional)

Birthday Stars

Design by DEANNA HUTCHISON

Cut dark blue card stock 7 x 5½ inches; score and fold in half. Tear light blue card stock approximately 5¼ x 3¼ inches. Use a computer or hand-print "Happy Birthday" on vellum and cut a rectangle around words. Attach rectangle toward bottom of light blue piece using two silver brads; adhere to card.

Center and adhere a 3½ x ½-inch silver strip onto card; punch three stars from silver card stock and run them through paper crimper. Cut three 1¼-inch squares from dark blue card stock; attach one crimped star to each square with an adhesive foam dot. Using a sewing needle, poke two holes into each square across from each other; insert wire through holes and twist ends into loops. Glue squares on top of silver strip. ∎

MATERIALS

Card stock: dark blue, light blue and silver
Clear vellum
2 silver brads
Small hole punch
Star punch
Sewing needle
Thin silver craft wire
Paper crimper
Adhesive foam dots
Glue stick
Computer font (optional)

Birthday Blossoms

Design by SUSAN STRINGFELLOW

MATERIALS

Pre-scored white card

Peach and light blue
  patterned papers

Flower vellum sticker

Pink adhesive mesh

2 mini black brads

Assorted fibers

"Happy Birthday" rubber
  stamp

Black ink pad

Peach chalk-finish ink pad

Adhesive foam tape

Glue stick

Add peach chalk-finish ink to the edges of pre-scored card. Cut peach patterned paper 3⅛ x 4¼ inches; adhere to lower left corner. Cut blue patterned paper 2⅜ x 3⅛ inches; adhere to upper right corner. Cut a 2⅜-inch square of adhesive mesh and attach near the upper left corner overlapping patterned papers.

Attach vellum sticker to white card stock; cut out and attach to card using foam tape. Cut three 8-inch lengths of fibers; wrap around lower part of sticker and secure on each side with mini brads. Stamp "Happy Birthday" in lower right corner. ∎

SOURCES: Pre-scored card from Die Cuts with a View; patterned papers and vellum sticker from NRN Designs; adhesive mesh from Magic Mesh; rubber stamp and ink pad from Stampin' Up!; Stampa Rosa chalk-finish ink pad from Creative Beginnings.

Happy Birthday

Design by KATIE BOLDT

MATERIALS

5½ x 8½-inch brown card
  stock

Cream fiber

Leaf tag sticker

5 matching buttons

Letter stickers

Black fine-tip marker

Yellow gel pen

Adhesive dots

Baby powder

Score and fold card stock in half. Attach letter stickers on top of buttons to spell "happy." Apply a small amount of baby powder to the sticky part around the hole on the leaf tag sticker. *Note: This will allow the fiber to be inserted through the hole more easily without getting stuck.* Thread fiber through leaf tag; attach to left portion of card. Referring to photo for placement, adhere letter buttons to card with adhesive dots. Write "birthday" alongside leaf tag; fill in outlines with gel pen. ∎

SOURCES: Leaf tag sticker from Karen Foster Design; letter stickers from Chatterbox.

In Sympathy

Design by CHERYL BALL, *courtesy of Duncan*
DIAGRAMS ON PAGE 94

Cut a piece of vellum slightly larger than the opening in card; adhere to the backside of opening. Using pattern provided, cut an oval from vellum; layer onto pink patterned paper and cut around oval with decorative-edge scissors leaving a small border. Punch double holes into each side of vellum oval; thread ribbon through holes to join ovals together. Trim ribbon ends.

Attach layered die cut to front of card with adhesive foam squares; adhere layered oval to bottom of card. Transfer sympathy sentiment to oval. Embellish oval, rose die cut and vellum with dots of paper paint.

For inside, cut a 2¾ x 3-inch rectangle from vellum; layer onto pink patterned paper and trim edges leaving a small border. Transfer desired sentiment to vellum; attach remaining layered rose die cut. ■

SOURCES: PSX card, layered die cuts, rub-on transfers, paper paint, vellum and patterned paper from Duncan.

MATERIALS

Blank iridescent white card with a window opening
Pink patterned paper
Clear vellum
2 layered rose die cuts
Sympathy sentiment rub-on transfers
Iridescent dimensional paper paint: green, white and pink
Sheer white ribbon
Double-slot punch
Adhesive foam squares
Glue stick
Decorative-edge scissors

Thinking of You

Design by CHERYL BALL, *courtesy of Duncan*

Cut a 3 x 4-inch piece of blue patterned paper and mount onto a 3½ x 4½-inch piece of purple floral patterned paper; glue to center of card front. Cut a small tag shape from white card stock; cut small pieces of patterned papers. Layer papers on top of tag; transfer desired sentiment rub-on to tag.

Arrange flower die cuts into a bouquet-like pattern on center of card front. Cut floss and glue tops down to create stems; attach flowers to stems. Tie tag to bottom of stems and attach a ribbon bow. Glue down ends of stems. Add light blue paper paint to tag; add dots and lines of paper to flowers and card. ■

SOURCES: PSX card, flower die cuts, paper paint, rub-on transfer, patterned papers and glue stick from Duncan.

MATERIALS

5½-inch square white card
Adhesive flower die cuts
Sentiment rub-on transfer
Purple floral patterned paper
Blue patterned paper
White card stock
Light blue paper paint
Green cotton floss
⅛-inch hole punch
Sheer ribbon
Paper cutter
Glue stick

Touch a Life

Design by HEATHER D. WHITE

MATERIALS

Brown card stock
Dictionary-print patterned
    paper
Brown patterned paper
Clear vellum
Brown and neutral fibers
4 brown mini square brads
Hole punch
Adhesive dots
Computer font (optional)

Cut brown card stock 5½ x 8½ inches; score and fold in half. Cut a 5½ x 4¼-inch piece of dictionary-print patterned paper; adhere to card front. Cut a 4¼ x 2-inch piece of brown patterned paper; adhere to top portion of card lining up edges. Trim edges even.

Punch a hole in seam of card toward top; thread several fibers through hole and wrap around card tying into a bow on front.

Use a computer or hand-print "to teach is to touch a life forever" onto vellum; cut a square around words. Mount vellum onto brown patterned paper; trim edges. Mount again onto brown card stock; trim edges. Attach a mini brad into each corner of vellum; attach layered piece to card over fibers with adhesive dots. ■

SOURCES: Patterned papers from Rusty Pickle; brads from All My Memories.

Thanks Coach

Design by ALISON BERGQUIST, *courtesy of PM Designs*

MATERIALS

White and light blue card
    stock
Red striped paper
Navy blue paint strip
Pre-colored baseball block
White fibers
Alphabet rubber stamps
Black ink pad
Glue pen
Adhesive dots

Cut red striped paper 5½ x 8½ inches; score and fold in half. Center and adhere paint strip to card. Tear two thin strips of light blue card stock; adhere one strip facedown above paint strip and adhere remaining strip facedown below paint strip. Trim ends even with card. Using glue pen, adhere a piece of white fiber to each torn strip.

Stamp "thanks coach" onto white card stock; tear around each word and adhere to card. Attach pre-colored baseball block to lower right corner of card with adhesive dots. ■

SOURCES: Paint strip and pre-colored block from PM Designs; rubber stamps from Delta/Rubber Stampede; paper and card stock from Chatterbox; glue pen from EK Success.

Wonderful Friend

Design by LEE MCKENNEY

Use decorative-edge scissors to cut off ½ inch from right edge of card. Cut a 1 x 7-inch strip from white card stock; cut one edge with decorative-edge scissors. Adhere to inside right edge of card lining up straight edges.

Push out the squares from the photo overlay. Use the stipple brush and opalescent light blue ink to add color to overlay; let dry. Cut a 3½ x 6-inch rectangle from patterned paper; adhere overlay on top of patterned paper. Adhere layered piece to front of card.

Use the watermark ink pad to stamp "To A Wonderful Friend" beneath image; emboss with silver embossing powder. Attach photo corner stickers at each corner; adhere dragonfly sticker to card. ■

SOURCES: Patterned paper and dimensional dragonfly sticker from K&Company; photo overlay from Die Cuts with a View; ink pads from Tsukineko; rubber stamp from Hero Arts; PSX embossing powder from Duncan; double-sided tape from Magic Scraps.

MATERIALS

5 x 7-inch blue card

Light blue and white card stock

12 x 12-inch blue floral patterned paper

Coordinating dragonfly dimensional sticker

4 x 6-inch white pre-cut photo overlay

Blue layered photo corner stickers

Watermark ink pad

Opalescent light blue ink pad

"To A Wonderful Friend" rubber stamp

Silver embossing powder

Embossing heat tool

Stipple brush

Decorative-edge scissors

¼-inch-wide double-sided tape

MATERIALS

Dark purple and light
    purple card stock
Light purple patterned
    paper
Dark purple and light
    purple embroidery floss
Beaded heart
    embellishment
Sandpaper
Adhesive foam tape
Glue stick
Computer font (optional)

Celebrate Life

Design by DEANNA HUTCHISON

Cut dark purple card stock 8½ x 5½ inches; score and fold in half. Cut patterned paper 3¾ x 5 inches; crumple and sand lightly. Smooth out piece and adhere to a 4 x 5¼-inch rectangle of light purple card stock.

Wrap dark purple embroidery floss three times around left side of layered rectangle leaving ¼-inch between each wrap. Repeat with light purple embroidery floss. Cinch floss together 1½ inches from top; attach beaded heart on top of cinched floss.

Use a computer or hand-print the following words onto light purple card stock: "LIVE," "DANCE," "SING" and "LOVE." Trim words and mount onto dark purple card stock. Trim edges; adhere to card with foam tape. ■

Each Moment is a Gift

Design by LEE MCKENNEY

Attach tulle over light purple paper by placing a piece of double-sided tape in the lower right corner. Cut dark purple paper in half diagonally from corner to corner; adhere one half to bottom right portion of layered light purple piece. Line up bottom and side edges; adhere to square card.

Cut a ½ x 11-inch strip of gold metallic paper; center and position onto layered papers corner to corner. Referring to photo, miter cut the corners to fit edges.

Attach large butterfly frame sticker to center of card; adhere heart clip in top right corner with clear-drying glue. Attach small flower stickers in bottom left corner. Attach word sticker to dark purple card stock; trim edges and attach to bottom right corner. ■

SOURCES: Metallic paper from Stampin' Up!; stickers from K&Company; heart clip from Making Memories.

MATERIALS

5 x 7-inch white card
5 x 7-inch dark purple paper
5 x 7-inch light purple paper
5 x 7-inch tulle with gold dots
Gold metallic paper
Dark purple card stock
"Each Moment is a Gift" sticker
Large round butterfly frame and small flower stickers
Gold heart clip
Double-sided tape
Clear-drying glue

Autumn Elegance

Design by SUSAN STRINGFELLOW

MATERIALS

Copper and navy blue
  card stock
Copper textured paper
Blue mesh
Decorative square rubber
  stamp
Iridescent clear embossing
  powder
Watermark ink pad
Copper rub-on paint
2 mini copper brads
Blue and copper fibers
Heat embossing tool
Foam mounting tape

Cut copper card stock 5½ x 8½ inches; score and fold in half. Use watermark ink pad to stamp decorative square image randomly on card front. Stamp image once onto navy blue card stock; emboss with iridescent embossing powder. Rub surface with metallic copper paint. Cut out image and mount onto copper textured paper; tear bottom edge. Wrap blue and copper fibers around bottom portion of textured paper.

Roughly cut a piece of blue mesh; attach to center of card. Adhere assembled image on top of mesh with mounting tape. Cut two small squares and two larger squares from navy blue card stock; apply copper rub-on paint to smaller squares. Adhere small squares to larger squares off center; attach squares in bottom left corner with copper mini brads. ■

SOURCES: Rubber stamp from Stampa Rosa; rub-on paint from Craf-T Products; watermark ink pad from Tsukineko.

Shades of Autumn

Design by SUSAN HUBER

MATERIALS

Orange card stock
Green patterned paper
Orange and green fibers
Gold leafing pen
Leaf button
Wire cutters
Glue stick
Adhesive dots

Cut orange card stock 5½ x 8½ inches; score and fold in half. Cut green patterned paper 5¼ x 4 inches; adhere to card. Cut a 1¾-inch square from orange card stock; apply gold to edges with leafing pen. Glue square toward bottom right corner of card. Wrap fibers around card; tie into a knot at edge of orange square. Remove shank from button with wire cutters; attach to orange square with adhesive dots. ■

SOURCES: Gold leafing pen from Krylon; leaf button from Jesse James & Co.

Falling Leaves

Design by DEANNA HUTCHISON

Cut orange card stock 4 x 7 inches; score and fold in half. Cut patterned paper 4 x 3½ inches; hold to front of card and tear off ½-inch from the bottom of both papers. ***Note:*** *Do not attach patterned paper to card at this point.*

Punch three leaves from brown and olive green card stock; lightly apply brown chalk to each leaf. Adhere one leaf toward upper right corner of patterned paper; center and attach adhesive mesh.

Wrap brown embroidery floss around left side of patterned paper twice; wrap green floss once. Secure ends in back with glue.

Referring to photo for placement, use green floss to sew three buttons to paper. Adhere remaining leaves on mesh. Glue assembled piece to card lining up edges. ∎

MATERIALS

Card stock: orange, brown and olive green
Orange patterned paper
Green adhesive mesh
Green and brown embroidery floss
Sewing needle
Leaf punch
Brown chalk
Buttons: green, red and orange
Glue stick

Summer Reprise

Design by DEANNA HUTCHISON

Cut dark green card stock 5¼ x 8 inches; score and fold in half. Cut patterned paper 3 x 4 inches; crumple up and sand. Mount onto gray card stock; tear edges and apply brown chalk to edges. Attach eyelet in bottom right corner; thread fibers through eyelet.

Use a computer or hand-print "Autumn is a second summer, where every leaf is a" onto gray card stock;

cut a 3½ x 2-inch rectangle around words. Apply brown chalk to edges. Attach photo corners to word rectangle; rub metallic gold chalk on corners. Adhere at an angle on top of crumpled paper.

Use a computer or hand-print "FLOWER" onto gray card stock; tear edges around word. Crumple up word and apply brown chalk to surface; glue to olive green card stock and trim edges. Attach safety pin at top of word; adhere to layered papers with adhesive foam tape. Glue assembled piece to card. ∎

MATERIALS

Card stock: dark olive green, olive green and gray
Olive green patterned paper
Gold safety pin
4 black photo corners
Metallic gold and brown chalk
Coordinating fibers
Eyelet
Sandpaper
Hole punch
Adhesive foam tape
Computer font (optional)

Happy Harvest

Design by MARY AYRES

MATERIALS

Card stock: red, tan, green, yellow, light brown and medium brown
Yellow envelope
Rusty tin wire
Jute
⅛-inch eyelet setter
3 (⅛-inch) round antique eyelets
Burlap strand
Permanent fabric adhesive
Red and white dye ink pads
Craft sponge
Rotary tool with scoring blade
Circle cutter
⁹⁄₁₆-inch circle punch
Decorative-edge scissors
Cellophane tape
Computer font (optional)

Cut tan card stock 7 x 10 inches; score and fold in half. Cut medium brown card stock 3½ x 5 inches; draw a pencil line horizontally across rectangle ¼ inch from top. Cut vertical slits in rectangle ⅜ inch apart, being careful not to cut above line.

Cut seven ⅜ x 4½-inch strips from light brown card stock and weave them in horizontally through slits in medium brown rectangle. Place cellophane tape around woven edges on back. Trim paper edges even with woven rectangle, being careful not to cut ¼-inch strip at top of rectangle. Round corners of basket and glue down ends of top strips.

Cut a ½ x 3¾-inch strip from light brown card stock; wrap burlap strand around piece with even spacing, gluing ends on back. Glue strip across top of woven rectangle and attach eyelets to both ends. Insert ends of a 10-inch piece of wire through eyelets and twist ends back around wire to form handle.

Use a computer or hand-print "happy harvest" on yellow card stock; cut a ¾ x 2¾-inch rectangle around words, leaving ½-inch of space on right side. Clip right corners of rectangle to make tag; attach eyelet and insert a 2½-inch piece of wire through eyelet in tag and eyelet on right side of basket and twist ends together. Glue tag to basket.

Cut six 4-inch diameter circles from red card stock. Using craft sponge, rub a small amount of cherry red ink on edges of circles and rub a highlighted area of white ink to top of circles. Cut six ⅝-inch pieces of jute and glue to top of circles.

Punch three ⁹⁄₁₆-inch diameter circles from green card stock; cut circles in half, using decorative-edge scissors, and glue to sides of stems. Glue five apples to top back of basket; glue entire piece to front of card. Glue remaining apple to upper left corner of envelope. ■

SOURCES: Fabric-Tac permanent adhesive from Beacon.

Vintage Grapes

DIAGRAMS ON PAGE 91

Design courtesy of P E B E O

MATERIALS

Transparent water-based
glass paint: golden
brown, olive green and
purple

Black outliner tube
transparent water-
based glass paint

Watercolor paper

Card stock: white, olive
green and brown

Acetate

Green sheer ribbon

Paintbrush

Paint palette

Hole punch

Glue stick

Paper towel

Project note: When using the black outliner tube, first unscrew the black nozzle and pop a hole in the metal tube. Replace the nozzle and squeeze the tube gently. Practice technique first on a paper towel.

Place acetate over the grape pattern; outline grapes with the black outliner glass paint. Outline a few extra random grape sections but do not connect them to large grape bunch. Repeat step with leaves pattern. Let dry for at least 15 minutes. Paint grapes purple. *Note: Paint in a circular motion allowing some areas to be lighter in appearance.* Paint leaves with both the olive green and golden brown paints to give the leaves a mottled effect. Allow to dry for one hour. Cut out grapes and leaves; place onto white card stock and adhere with glue stick. Cut out card stock along edges.

Lightly draw a small section of grapes and leaves onto watercolor paper; gently rip around the design to get a loose leaf shape. Paint the watercolor grapes and leaves; allow to dry and then outline a few grapes with black paint.

Fold a 6⅝ x 8-inch piece of watercolor paper in half. Paint the front with diluted golden brown glass paint; allow to dry. Use a heavy object to weigh down card to flatten.

Glue the watercolor paper grapes and leaves to card front with edges extending over card perimeter; glue acetate leaves onto card followed by the acetate grapes allowing pieces to overlap. Once completely dry, tie ribbon around the fold of the card and tie into a bow.

For small tag, repeat painting process for the plaid pattern provided and let dry. Adhere to white card stock and trim edges even. Cut a 1¼ x 6⅝-inch strip of white card stock; fold in half. Adhere plaid pattern to tag.

Create a matted look by cutting a 1¼ x 3¼-inch piece of olive green card stock; cut out an opening that allows the plaid pattern to show through. Adhere olive green frame on top of plaid piece. Cut a 1¼ x 3¼-inch piece of brown card stock and cut out an opening that allows plaid pattern to show through; adhere to tag. Punch a hole in top corner; thread ribbon through hole and tie a bow. Trim ends if needed. ∎

SOURCES: Vitrea 160 glass paints from Pebeo.

Masquerade

Design by SHARON REINHART

MATERIALS

Black linen and iridescent
    gold card stock
Red and purple suede
    paper
¼-inch-wide gold mesh
    curling ribbon
Red rhinestone shapes:
    star and marquis
4 (8mm) red rhinestones
2 black cabochons
Assorted green rhinestone
    shapes
2 E beads: purple and
    green
Green decorating foil
Watermark ink pad
Gold embossing powder
Star rubber stamp
Mask rubber stamp
Gold star button
Gold leafing pen
Red marker
Wood skewer
Adhesive dots
Adhesive mounting
    squares
Embossing heat tool
Shank removers
Bone folder
Tacky glue
Magnet
Paper crimper
Hole punch

RED INVITATION

Cut an 8 x 8½-inch piece of black linen card stock; score and fold in half. Cut a piece of gold card stock 4 x 4¼ inches and another piece 2 x 8½ inches. Ink star image and stamp randomly on 2 x 8½-inch piece; let dry and adhere ⅛ inch from right edge of card front.

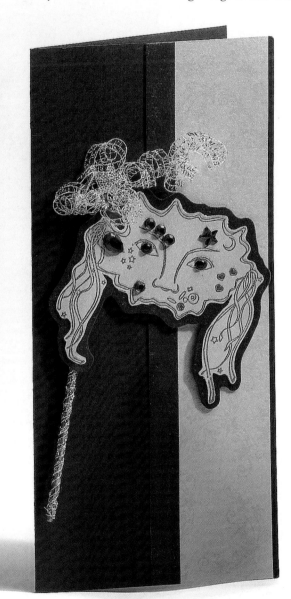

Cut a ½ x 8½-inch piece of red suede paper and adhere onto left edge of stamped gold piece. Stamp and emboss mask image onto 4 x 4¼-inch piece of gold card stock with gold embossing powder. Cut out mask image leaving a small border.

Adhere mask to red suede paper; cut out leaving approximately ¼-inch border. Attach rhinestones and cabochons to mask with adhesive dots; color in hearts and any other desired areas with marker.

Cut skewer to 5½ inches; color with gold leafing pen and let dry. Wrap ribbon around skewer and secure both ends with glue. Remove shank from star button and adhere to pointed end of skewer. Cut a 12-inch length of ribbon and tie in a knot below star; adhere skewer to back left side of mask with glue and adhere magnet to back of mask.

Punch 2 (⅛-inch) holes 2½ inches from top of card and 1 inch from folded edge; leave ⅛-inch distance between holes. Cut 14-inch length of ribbon; thread through holes and tie around skewer to secure mask to card.

PURPLE CARD

Cut an 8½ x 5½-inch piece of iridescent gold card stock; score and fold in half. Cut a 1½ x 5½-inch piece of purple suede paper; adhere to left side of card ½ inch from fold. Cut a ½ x 5½-inch piece of gold card stock; adhere to card ½ inch from left edge of purple suede.

Stamp and emboss mask image with gold powder on a 4 x 4¼-inch piece of gold card stock; cut out mask, making sure to leave a small border. Adhere mask to purple suede paper and cut out leaving ¼ inch border.

Cut a 1 x 3½-inch piece of green foil and run through crimping tool; form piece into a fan shape and adhere to embossed mask. Attach marquis shaped rhinestone to foil fan; adhere remaining rhinestones to mask.

Cut skewer to 4½ inches; color with gold leafing pen and let dry. Cut 2 (5-inch) lengths of ribbon and tie in a knot around skewer. Glue beads to pointed end of skewer; adhere to back of mask and attach mask to card with mounting squares. ■

SOURCES: Rubber stamps from Magenta and Paper Parachute; watermark ink pad from Tsukineko.

Halloween Confetti

Design by JULIE EBERSOLE

Cut orange card stock 5½ x 8½ inches; score and fold in half. Cut a 5½ x 2-inch strip of black card stock; tear long edges and adhere to card. Stamp bat image three times in upper right corner. Stamp "Happy Halloween" in lower right corner.

Cover the slide mount with orange patterned paper; cut an "x" through window portion. Fold and adhere the flaps around to the back; trim outside edges even with slide mount. Adhere a square of acetate to the backside of the slide making sure to cover opening. Attach four thin strips of foam mounting tape along the perimeter of the window on the backside. **Note:** *Do not leave any gaps between foam strips.* Stamp "Boo!" onto pale peach card stock; cut a rectangle around word large enough to cover back opening. Fill shaker with confetti and secure pale peach panel to foam tape with message showing through window. Press firmly to create a tight seal. Mount completed shaker to card. ■

SOURCES: Rubber stamps from A Muse Art Stamps.

MATERIALS

Card stock: orange, black and pale peach
Orange patterned paper
Rubber stamps: small bat, "Happy Halloween" and "Boo!"
Black ink pad
Slide mount
Acetate
Halloween-themed confetti
Craft knife
Adhesive foam mounting tape
Glue stick

Trick-or-Treat

Design by MARGARET HANSON-MADDOX

DIAGRAM ON PAGE 94

MATERIALS

Card stock: black, yellow
  and orange
Envelope template
Candy corn printed paper
Black fine-tip permanent
  marker
Decorative-edge scissors
Glue stick
Sucker

Cut a 4¾ x 5¾-inch piece of orange card stock; cut two ⅜-inch strips from scrapbook paper and glue on the left and top edges of orange piece, referring to photo for placement. Using decorative-edge scissors, cut around orange card stock, approximately ¼ inch from edge. Keep trimmings for envelope. Cut a 2-inch diameter circle from yellow card stock and glue in upper left corner of orange piece. Trace witch pattern on black card stock and cut out; lay sucker on card and glue witch over sucker stick. Using black marker, write "Trick or Treat" in lower right corner.

ENVELOPE

Using template, cut and create envelope from black card stock. Glue trimmings from card to lower left corner of envelope. ■

SOURCES: Printed paper from Hot Off The Press.

Batty Treats

Design by MARGARET HANSON-MADDOX

DIAGRAMS ON PAGE 94

MATERIALS

Black and white card stock
Envelope template
Silver and black gel pens
Printed lettering tags
Candy corn printed paper
12 inches ¹⁄₁₆-inch-wide
  orange satin ribbon
6 (4mm) wiggly eyes
2 orange eyelets
½-inch black self-stick
  letters
Paper punch
Cutting mat
Glue stick
Adhesive foam squares
2 sticks of gum

Trace bat pattern onto black card stock; cut out and add details with silver gel pen. Cut slits for gum inserts. Glue lettering tags to inside of both wings to spell out "BOO."

Trace ghost pattern onto white card stock; cut out ghosts and draw on eyebrows with black gel pen. Glue wiggly eyes on ghosts and bat; using foam squares, adhere ghosts to front of bat wings. Attach eyelets to bottom corners of wings; insert gum into slits. Glue center of ribbon on bottom end of bat's tail in back and thread through eyelets; tie in a bow.

ENVELOPE

Using template, cut and create envelope from black card stock. Cut a ⅞-inch-wide piece of scrapbook paper and glue ¼ inch from left side of envelope. Trace ghost pattern onto white card stock; add eyes and eyebrows with black gel pen. Adhere self-stick letters to scrapbook strip to spell out "BOO"; attach ghost. ■

SOURCES: Printed paper and lettering tags from Hot Off The Press; self-stick letters from U.S. Stamp & Sign.

Boo!

Design by ALISON BERGQUIST, *courtesy of PM Designs*

Cut a 5½ x 8½-inch piece of purple card stock; score and fold in half. Cut a 4 x 5¼-inch rectangle from black card stock; wrap white fiber randomly around rectangle and glue ends in back. Attach letter nail head embellishments in bottom right corner to spell "boo." Adhere ghost block to top portion of card stock weaving corners in and out through white fiber. Adhere assembled piece to card. ■

SOURCES: Pre-colored block from PM Designs

MATERIALS

Purple and black card
    stock
Thin white fiber
Pre-colored ghost block
Alphabet nail head
    embellishments
Glue stick

Black Cat

Design by JULIE EBERSOLE

Cut white card stock 5½ x 8½ inches; score and fold in half. Cut a 4¼ x 5½-inch rectangle from yellow card stock; adhere to card front. Cut a 2¾ x 2½-inch rectangle from white card stock; stamp concave rectangle onto piece with yellow ink. Referring to photo, stamp circle above rectangle with orange ink; stamp cat and Halloween sentiment with black ink. Mount stamped piece onto black card stock; mount layered piece to card. Attach star eyelets beneath stamped piece. Wrap black fiber through card; tie in front. ■

SOURCES: Rubber stamps from A Muse Art Stamps.

MATERIALS

Card stock: white, yellow
    and black
Rubber stamps: cat,
    "Happy Halloween,"
    circle and concave
    rectangle
Ink pads: orange, black
    and yellow
3 silver star eyelets
Black tinsel fiber
Glue stick
Hole punch

Happy Jack

Design by KATHLEEN PANEITZ

MATERIALS

White, black and pale
    orange card stock
Soft metal pewter
    embossing sheet
Metal pumpkin
    embellishment
Black fine-tip marker
Black gingham ribbon
Raffia
Typewriter
Double-sided adhesive
Adhesive foam squares

Cut white card stock 4 x 8⅛ inches; score and fold in half. Cut a 3¾-inch square from pale orange card stock; adhere to card. Insert a sheet of embossing metal into typewriter; type fall- and Halloween-related words onto the metal. Take metal out of typewriter and trim to 3¾ x 2½ inches; mat metal onto black card stock. Tear top and bottom edges; trim sides even with metal. Adhere ribbon around middle of metal; trim edges even and adhere to card.

Cut a 1½ x 1¾-inch rectangle from white card stock; outline edges with black marker. Using adhesive foam squares, attach metal pumpkin embellishment to rectangle. Referring to photo, attach rectangle to card. Tie a small raffia bow; adhere to ribbon. ∎

SOURCES: Metal embossing sheet from American Art Clay Co.; pumpkin embellishment from Pilgrim Imports Mailable Art.

Boo To You DIAGRAMS ON PAGE 90

Design by HELEN RAFSON

Cut a 4⅛ x 6⅛-inch piece of orange striped paper using decorative-edge scissors. Center and glue onto card; let dry. Draw small stitch markers around perimeter of orange paper.

Use patterns to trace the letters onto black card stock; cut out. Use white gel marker to draw small stitch markers around inside and outside edges of letters.

Use ⅝-inch circle punch and ¼-inch hole punch to punch two circles from black card stock. Dip toothpick into white paint and make two dots onto smaller circle to make spider eyes; let dry. Glue larger circle to smaller circle to form a spider; let dry.

Referring to photo, glue letters and spider to card. Draw legs onto spider and a line extending from top of paper to spider. Randomly glue moveable eyes to card; let dry.

SOURCES: Zip Dry paper adhesive from Beacon.

MATERIALS

5 x 7-inch white card
Tracing paper
Black card stock
Orange striped paper
Black fine-tip permanent
  marker
White gel marker
White acrylic paint
4 (12mm) moveable eyes
2 (15mm) moveable eyes
Decorative-edge scissors
¼-inch hole punch
⅜-inch circle punch
Toothpick
Instant-dry paper adhesive
Ruler

Autumn Thanks

Design by RENAE CURTZ, *courtesy of Stampin' Up!*

MATERIALS

Rubber stamps: small
    alphabet, small star,
    leaf outline and leaf
    shadow
Card stock: red, brown,
    light brown and
    natural
Ink pads: red, brown and
    light brown
Ivory grosgrain ribbon
Natural linen thread
Adhesive foam squares
Glue stick

Cut light brown card stock 5½ x 8½ inches; score and fold in half. Cut a 2⅝-inch-wide strip of brown card stock; adhere toward top portion of card. Cut a 2½-inch-wide strip of red card stock; use red ink to stamp small star image randomly onto strip. Adhere to brown card stock strip; trim edges even with card. Wrap grosgrain ribbon around card centered on the red strip; secure in the center.

Using red and brown inks, stamp leaf outline image three times across a 3½ x 1⅝-inch natural card stock rectangle. Referring to photo, alternate ink colors and angle of image for each leaf. Stamp the leaf shadow image over each leaf outline with light brown ink.

Layer stamped rectangle onto brown card stock; trim leaving a 1⁄16-inch border on the top, bottom and right side. Leave a ¼-inch border on left side; score and fold left side over. Wrap linen thread around folded border; tie in a small knot to secure. Center and attach to card with adhesive foam squares.

On both sides of stamped rectangle, tie a knot around grosgrain ribbon with a small piece of linen thread. Trim ends. Use brown ink to stamp "give thanks" in lower right corner. ■

SOURCES: Rubber stamps, card stock, ink pads, ribbon, linen thread and adhesive foam squares from Stampin' Up!

Gobble Gobble!

Design courtesy of PM DESIGNS

Cut brown flecked card stock 6 x 12 inches; score and fold in half. Cut a 6 x 2½-inch strip of light brown patterned paper and adhere to top of card.

Layer pre-colored turkey block onto black card stock; trim edges leaving a small border. Layer again on brown patterned paper; trim edges leaving a small border. Center and adhere layered image to card.

Referring to photo for placement, punch two holes on both sides of image on patterned paper; thread hemp cording through holes and tie into knots. Stamp "Gobble Gobble" onto twill tape along with a few small hearts; attach underneath image with gold brads. ■

SOURCES: Pre-color block from PM Designs; patterned papers from Paper Adventures and Doodlebug Design Inc.

MATERIALS

Brown flecked and black
    card stock
Brown and light brown
    patterned papers
Pre-colored turkey block
Hemp cord
Alphabet and small heart
    rubber stamps
Black ink pad
Twill tape
2 mini gold brads
Small hole punch
Glue stick

Give Thanks

Design by NANCY BILLETDEAUX

Score and fold white card stock in half. Cut green patterned paper 8½ x 11 inches; score and fold in half. Place over white card stock and adhere. Cut a 7½ x 4½-inch piece of fall leaves patterned paper; attach an eyelet in each corner. Cut green fiber in half to make two 8-inch pieces; thread one fiber through the top eyelets and secure ends in back with glue. Thread remaining fiber through bottom eyelets and secure ends in back.

Cut ten 1-inch squares from orange patterned paper; stamp a different letter on each square to spell "GIVE THANKS." Referring to photo, glue each square in place. Attach an eyelet at the center top of each square; glue assembled piece to card.

For envelope, trace envelope flap onto green patterned paper and cut out. Adhere to flap. Cut a ½ x 8¾-inch strip of fall leaves patterned paper; center and adhere to flap. ■

SOURCES: Patterned papers from Provo Craft; rubber stamps from Hero Arts.

MATERIALS

8½ x 11-inch white card
    stock
5¾ x 8¾-inch white
    envelope
12 x 12-inch patterned
    papers: green, orange
    and fall leaves
Large alphabet rubber
    stamps
Black ink pad
16 inches green sparkle
    fiber
14 (⅛-inch) silver eyelets
Eyelet setting tool
Craft knife
Glue

Because I Care

Design by J O D I   J O H N S O N, *courtesy of Stampin' Up!*

MATERIALS

- 8½ x 5½-inch navy card stock
- 2⅜ x 4-inch green card stock
- 4 x 5½-inch light brown and white card stock
- Navy and green ink pads
- Sentiment rubber stamp
- Flower and starburst rubber stamps
- Natural hemp cord
- Light brown eyelets
- Eyelet setting tool
- Small hammer
- Hole punch
- Large square punch
- Adhesive foam dots

Score and fold navy card stock in half. Ink starburst image with green ink and stamp onto green card stock; carefully tear bottom of green card stock. Cut a 2½ x 3¾-inch piece of light brown card stock and adhere green piece on top of light brown piece; attach layered piece to center of navy card.

Ink flower image with navy ink and stamp image onto white card stock; clean flower stamp and ink image with green ink onto white card stock. Once dry, cut out navy flower and center of green flower, leaving a small border around all edges.

Punch a square from light brown card stock and adhere navy flower on top of square; attach green center to flower with adhesive foam dot. Dot may need to be trimmed to fit shape of flower's center.

Attach piece to top section of green and light brown piece centered on card.

Ink sentiment stamp with navy ink onto a 3¾ x ½-inch piece of white card stock; place eyelets on each end and secure.

Adhere sentiment piece below flower image; run hemp cord through eyelets, wrap cord around back of card and tie cord in a bow on left front side. ■

SOURCES: Card stock, ink pads, eyelets, hemp cord, jumbo square punch and rubber stamps from Stampin' Up!.

Taking Time Out

Design by DEBBIE RINES, *courtesy of Duncan*

Cut light peach card stock 5⅜-inch square; cut purple patterned paper 5¼ inches square. Layer squares together and adhere to card. Cut a 2 x 2¾-inch rectangle from light purple vellum; transfer desired sentiment to vellum and glue rectangle to lower right corner of card.

Cut four strips of ribbon to fit each side of the card; position in place to form a frame around card and attach with brads in each corner. Tie a bow with another piece of ribbon and glue to vellum. Attach layered die cuts; add dots of paper paint to the leaves and flowers.

For inside of card, cut a rectangle from vellum and layer on top of a rectangle cut from purple patterned paper. Adhere inside card; transfer desired sentiment to vellum. Attach a layered flower die cut in corner. ∎

SOURCES: PSX square card, layered die cuts, paper paint, glue stick, rub-on transfers, patterned paper, vellum and mini brads from Duncan.

MATERIALS

5½-inch square white card
Pre-embellished layered flower die cuts
Light purple vellum
Purple patterned paper
Light peach card stock
Opalescent white paper paint
Sentiment rub-on transfers
4 mini gold brads
Sheer white ribbon
Paper trimmer
Glue stick

Taking time out to send you warm wishes

Dream

Design by SHARON REINHART

MATERIALS

Black and white card stock
White mulberry paper
White paper
Black ink pad
Rubber stamps: alphabet
   set, world, window
   screen background and
   dream motif
5 mini black brads
Black nylon screening
1/16-inch hole punch
Small circle punch
Bone folder
Adhesive foam tape
Glue stick

Cut black card stock 4¼ x 11 inches; score and fold in half. Cut a 4¼ x 5½-inch rectangle from white paper; stamp world, dream motif and window screen background images randomly on surface leaving some white areas. Tear edges and adhere to card; fold and adhere top overlapping edge to back of card.

Tear two small pieces of mulberry paper; adhere to upper left and right sides of card. Fold and adhere overlapping edges inside card.

Cut five 1 x ¾-inch rectangles from white card stock; cut top corners to create tag shapes. Stamp window screen image onto each tag; stamp a letter on each to spell out "DREAM." Punch a 1/16-inch hole at top of each tag; insert black brad. Referring to photo for placement, adhere tags to card using adhesive foam tape.

Stamp dream motif image twice onto white paper; punch out a small image from each motif with the circle punch. Cut two ¾ x 1⅛-inch rectangles from nylon screen; adhere to upper left and bottom right corners of card by attaching adhesive foam tape to circle images and positioning screen pieces between card and foam tape. ■

SOURCES: Rubber stamps from Plaid/All Night Media, Magenta, Hero Arts and Uptown Design Co.

Inspire

Design by LEE MCKENNEY

Cut dark blue card stock 5 x 7 inches; cut light blue card stock 5 x 7 inches. Cut light blue card stock in half diagonally. Punch the upper left corner of the dark blue card stock with heart punch; with the same punch, repeat in the lower right corner of the light blue card stock. Adhere the light blue card stock to the dark blue lining up edges. Cut a 4½ x 6½-inch rectangle from butterfly patterned paper making sure to include a butterfly in rectangle; insert rectangle into the punched corner pockets of the layered card stock. Adhere assembled piece to card.

Attach rice paper pocket to front of card at an angle; center and apply the "Inspire" sticker to pocket.

For tag, cut a 1¾ x 4-inch piece of dark blue card stock; cut top corners off to form a tag shape. Cut a 1⅜ x 3¾-inch piece of butterfly patterned paper; cut off top corners to form a tag and adhere to card stock tag.

Punch a hole at top of tag. Fold blue fiber in half; insert through hole and thread ends through formed loop. Trim ends if needed. Tie dragonfly charm to one of the fibers. Insert tag into rice paper pocket. ∎

SOURCES: Paper punches from McGill Craftivity Inc.; rice paper pocket and fiber from EK Success; word sticker from Bo-Bunny Press.

MATERIALS

5 x 7-inch blank white card
Dark blue and light blue card stock
Blue butterfly patterned paper
Heart corner punch
³⁄₁₆-inch hole punch
"Inspire" clear sticker
20 inches blue fiber
Small silver dragonfly charm
Small rice paper pocket with printed leaf
Double-sided tape

DIAGRAMS ON PAGE 92

Happy Hanukkah

Design by A M Y Y I N G L I N G, *courtesy of Stampin' Up!*

MATERIALS

Rubber stamps: Star
    of David, "Happy
    Hanukkah" and
    "my friend"
Blue and light blue
    card stock
White mulberry paper
Watermark ink pad
Black solvent-based
    ink pad
Clear embossing powder
Embossing heat tool
⅜-inch-wide white
    organdy ribbon
Silver cord
Small silver round
    metal tag
Sewing machine and
    white sewing thread
Adhesive foam squares
Glue stick

Cut light blue card stock 5½ x 8½ inches; score and fold in half. Cut a 5½ x 4-inch rectangle from light blue card stock; crumple piece and carefully smooth it out. Use watermark ink pad to stamp "Happy Hanukkah" onto crumpled piece and emboss with clear embossing powder; machine-sew to front of card.

Using black solvent-based ink, stamp "my friend" onto metal tag and thread onto silver cording. Wrap silver cord and organdy ribbon around card; tie into a knot on right side of card securing metal tag.

Use watermark ink pad to stamp Star of David image onto light blue card stock; emboss with clear embossing powder. Trim around image and layer onto blue card stock; trim again leaving a small blue border. Layer onto white mulberry paper and attach to card with adhesive foam squares. ■

Sources: Rubber stamps, embossing powder, card stock, metal tag and adhesive foam dots from Stampin' Up!; watermark ink pad from Hero Arts; solvent-based ink pad from Tsukineko.

Menorah Card

Design by M A R Y A Y R E S

MATERIALS

White, blue and dark blue
    card stock
Sewing machine with silver
    sewing thread
1⅛ x 2⅛-inch silver book
    plate
⅛-inch-wide blue silk
    ribbon
24 (⅛-inch) round silver
    eyelets
11 small round silver brads
Instant-dry paper adhesive
1/16- and ⅛-inch circle
    punches
Rotary tool and scoring
    blade
Dark blue marker (optional)
Computer font (optional)

Cut blue card stock 8 x 10 inches; score and fold in half. Machine-stitch around card front ⅛-inch from edge. Cut a 4½ x 7½-inch rectangle from dark blue card stock; center and adhere to card. Cut a 4¼ x 7¼-inch rectangle from white card stock. Cut two 1½-inch squares from blue card stock; cut each in half to form four triangles. Glue triangles to corners of white rectangle. Machine-stitch around triangles ⅛ inch from edge.

For menorah, punch ⅛-inch holes in white rectangle at open circles indicated on pattern; attach eyelets. Insert ribbon in and out through eyelets, following lines on pattern; glue ends in back to secure.

Punch 1/16-inch holes in white rectangle at dots indicated on pattern; attach brads. Center and adhere white rectangle to dark blue rectangle.

Use a computer or hand-print "Happy Hanukkah" on blue card stock with dark blue ink; cut a rectangle around words and glue to back of book plate. Position book plate underneath menorah and mark placement of holes; punch 1/16-inch holes at marks. Attach book plate to card placing brads in holes. ■

SOURCES: Zip Dry paper adhesive from Beacon.

Warm Winter Wishes

Design by PAM HORNSCHU, *courtesy of Stampendous*

Use opalescent light purple and opalescent light blue ink pads to apply color directly to card in color blocks; use opalescent blue ink to stamp snowflake image randomly over card. Referring to photo, stamp chick, hat and message onto white tag; color with pencils.

Stamp snowflake image randomly around edge of tag using opalescent light purple ink.

Apply heat-puff paint around base of chick and on hat; draw some tiny snowballs with paint. Sprinkle paint with glitter; heat to puff.

Punch two holes ¼-inch apart at top of tag; loop ribbons through tag from front to back. Cross ribbons over each other and thread back through opposite holes; trim ends. Attach tag to card with adhesive foam squares. ■

SOURCES: Rubber stamps, ink pads, note card, tag, heat-puff paint, glitter, watercolor pencils and adhesive foam squares from Stampendous.

MATERIALS

White note card
White tag
Rubber stamps: solid block, snowflake, chick, small winter hat, "Warm Winter Wishes"
Ink pads: black, opalescent light purple, opalescent light blue and opalescent blue
Watercolor pencils
Purple and sheer ribbons
White heat-puff paint
Heat tool
Extra-fine glitter
Hole punch
Adhesive foam squares

Hearts Come Home

Design by ILENE ALBERT-NELSON, *courtesy of Shortcuts/Paramount Brands*

Cut dark green card stock 5½ x 8½ inches; score and fold in half. Cut gold mulberry paper 4 x 5¼ inches; adhere to card. Cut a 1½ x 4½-inch strip of dark green card stock; attach star eyelets evenly spaced across center. Punch eight holes across top of strip; alternate threading holes with ribbons and fiber. Tie each into a knot; trim ends. Attach embellished strip to card with adhesive foam tape. Use a computer or hand-print desired message on mulberry paper; cut rectangle around message and adhere inside card. ■

SOURCES: Mulberry paper from Shortcuts/Paramount Brands; star eyelets from Making Memories.

MATERIALS

Dark green card stock
Gold mulberry paper
Green gingham ribbon
Green sheer ribbon
Olive green fiber
3 medium silver star eyelets
Hole punch
Adhesive foam tape
Double-sided tape
Computer font (optional)

Happy Holiday Wishes

Design by RENAE CURTZ, *courtesy of Stampin' Up!*

MATERIALS

Card stock: red, blue, olive
    green, light brown and
    white
Small white tag
Rubber stamps: Christmas
    tree, snowman snow
    globe and "Happy
    Holiday Wishes"
Ink pads: red, olive green,
    light green, golden
    yellow, light brown,
    blue, brown and black
Watercolor brush
Neutral-color button
Natural linen thread
Sewing needle
Adhesive foam squares
Glue stick

Cut red card stock 5½ x 8½ inches; score and fold in half. Use red ink to stamp snowman snow globe image repeatedly across bottom edge of card. Cut a ⅞ x 8½-inch strip of light brown card stock; center and adhere to front and back of card.

Cut a 2⅛ x 3¼-inch rectangle of white card stock; use black ink to stamp Christmas tree image onto rectangle. Apply color to image using ink pads and watercolor brush.

Cut olive green card stock 2½ x 3½ inches; crumple up and gently smooth out. Layer colored tree image onto crumpled rectangle. Layer onto a 2¾ x 4¼-inch rectangle of blue card stock; tear bottom edge of rectangle. Attach to card with adhesive foam squares.

Crinkle up bottom edge of white tag; stamp holiday message on tag with red ink. Insert linen thread through tag and button; sew button to light brown strip. Tie thread into a knot. Secure tag with an adhesive foam square. ■

SOURCES: Rubber stamps, card stock, ink pads, linen thread and adhesive foam squares from Stampin' Up!.

Holiday Carol

Design by KATHLEEN PANEITZ

MATERIALS

Green textured card stock
Holly berry patterned
    paper
Pewter holly berry sticker
Metal-edge square vellum
    tag
Metallic color rub-on
    paints
Sponge-tip applicators
Red raffia
Glue stick

Cut green textured card stock 5¼ x 8½ inches; score and fold in half. Cut a 2½-inch strip of holly berry patterned paper; adhere to card. Trim edges even. Attach holly berry sticker to vellum tag. Using metallic rub-on paints and sponge-tip applicators, add color to sticker. Wrap raffia around top portion of card twice; insert raffia through vellum tag and tie into a bow. Trim ends and adhere tag to card to secure. ■

SOURCES: Patterned paper from Penny Black Inc.; metal-edge tag from Making Memories; sticker from Magenta; rub-on paints from Craf-T Products.

Snowflake Celebration

Design by SHAUNA BERGLUND-IMMEL, *courtesy of Hot Off The Press*

Adhere a piece of blue patterned paper to card front; trim edges even with card. Cut a 2¼ x 6½-inch piece of snowflake-patterned paper; layer onto white textured paper and trim leaving a ¹⁄₁₆-inch border on right side. Line up edges on left side of card and adhere.

Use watermark ink pad to apply ink to card edges; sprinkle white embossing powder on inked areas and emboss.

Cut white textured paper to fit onto front of slide mount and adhere; cut out opening. Mat slide mount onto blue patterned paper; trim edges to ¹⁄₁₆-inch. Frame the pre-embossed snowflake inside slide mount. Referring to photo for placement, wrap navy blue ribbon around both sides of slide mount; secure with small pinwheel eyelets and brads. Adhere to card; wrap ends of ribbon around inside and back. Glue ends to secure.

Mat small tag onto white textured paper; trim edges ¹⁄₁₆-inch. Stamp "OY" using alphabet rubber stamps and watermark ink pad; emboss with white embossing powder. Attach tag to upper right corner of card with a mini brad and pinwheel eyelet. Tie a bow with ribbon and attach above tag with an adhesive dot. ■

SOURCES: Papers, ribbon, pre-emboss snowflake, slide mount, pinwheel eyelets and brads from Hot Off The Press; watermark ink pad from Tsukineko; rubber stamps from Hero Arts.

MATERIALS
5 x 6½-inch white card
Texture papers: snowflake, blue patterned and white
Small coordinating tag with "J" printed on it
Navy blue ribbon
Pre-embossed snowflake
Square slide mount
3 small silver pinwheel eyelets
3 small silver round brads
Watermark ink pad
White embossing powder
Alphabet rubber stamps
Heat embossing tool
Craft knife
Adhesive dots

Holly Leaves

Design by MELINDA JOHNSON, *courtesy of Clearsnaps*

Apply clear embossing ink directly from the bottle onto the holly leaf rubber stamp wheel; ink wheel well. Insert wheel into handle; roll holly leaf image across red card stock at an angle. Emboss leaves with gold embossing powder.

Stamp "Season's Greetings" onto navy blue card stock with clear embossing ink pad; emboss with gold embossing powder. Trim a square around words and attach to bottom right corner of card with an adhesive foam square. ■

SOURCES: Rubber stamp from Hero Arts; embossing ink and ink pad, rubber stamp wheel and handle from Clearsnap.

MATERIALS
5½-inch square navy blue card stock
5¼-inch square red card stock
Holly berry leaf rubber stamp wheel
Rubber stamp wheel handle
"Season's Greetings" rubber stamp
Embossing ink pad
Bottle of clear embossing ink
Gold embossing powder
Clear embossing ink pad
Adhesive foam squares
Glue stick

O' Christmas Tree

Design by SHARON REINHART

MATERIALS

Dark green card stock
Dark green suede paper
Opalescent gold paper
¼-inch-wide gold ribbon
Clear glitter glue
Christmas tree brass
    stencil
"Happy Holidays" brass
    stencil
Embossing stylus
Light box or light source
Decorative corner punch
⅛-inch hole punch
Double-sided tape
Removable tape
Wax paper

Cut dark green card stock 5½ x 8½ inches; score and fold in half. Cut opalescent gold paper 2⅝ x 3¹⁄₁₆ inches; center and secure Christmas tree stencil to paper with removable tape. Place stencil onto light source sandwiching stencil between light source and paper. Rub paper with wax paper. ***Note:*** *This allows the stylus to glide smoothly.* Trace the perimeter of the stencil and all open motifs; press stylus gently into edge of stencil for sharp images. Remove paper from stencil.

Punch two ⅛-inch holes ½ inch apart directly below tree image. Cut a 3-inch length of gold ribbon; insert ribbon through holes from front to back. Cross ribbon in back and insert back through opposite holes to return both ends to the front; trim ends.

Layer embossed piece onto a 3 x 4-inch green suede rectangle; use decorative corner punch to embellish each corner. Layer piece onto a 3⅛ x 4⅛-inch opalescent gold rectangle; adhere to card. Apply a small amount of glitter glue to random areas of embossed motif; let dry.

For inside, use "Happy Holidays" stencil and opalescent gold paper to create an embossed message. Follow instructions above for embossing. Once message is embossed, cut a rectangle around words and adhere. ■

SOURCES: Brass stencil from Lasting Impressions for Paper, Inc.; corner punch from Uchida of America.

MATERIALS

Nativity scene rubber
    stamp
Crackle-pattern
    background rubber
    stamp
Brown instant-dry ink pad
Colored pencils
Ivory and ivory speckled
    card stock
Alphabet and ribbon card
    stock stickers
Adhesive foam dots

Rustic Winter Wishes

Design by JUDI KAUFFMAN

Cut ivory speckled card stock 5½ x 8½ inches; score and fold in half. Using brown ink, stamp crackle-pattern background image onto card front.

Stamp nativity scene onto ivory card stock with brown ink; let dry and add color to image with colored pencils. Cut a 5 x 1⅞-inch rectangle around image.

Layer ribbon stickers onto card; attach alphabet stickers to spell "JOY" at card bottom. Use adhesive foam dots to attach nativity scene image. ■

SOURCES: Rubber stamp from Red Castle; ink pad from Tsukineko; stickers from Pebbles Inc.

Wonderful Wishes

Design by DEBBIE RINES, *courtesy of Duncan*

Fold green card stock in half; with fold on left side, cut a 1-inch strip off right side on top layer only. Cut a 5 x 8-inch piece of printed paper; cut a piece of ribbon and adhere to right side of printed paper. Fold edges of ribbon over to back of paper and glue paper inside card so strip of ribbon shows when card is closed.

Stamp poinsettia and Christmas sentiment images to red card stock; let dry. Cut stamped areas with decorative-edge scissors. Layer stamped pieces onto green card stock; cut with decorative-edge scissors. Layer pieces onto printed paper; cut with decorative-edge scissors. Layer pieces onto mulberry paper and tear edges. Glue assembled pieces to card front.

Squeeze drops of paper glaze to centers of poinsettias; cover with gold beads and, once dry, remove excess beads. Apply the paper glaze to poinsettia petals and to Christmas sentiment; let dry. ∎

SOURCES: Aleene's Paper Glaze, Aleene's Memory Glue, PSX printed paper, mulberry paper and rubber stamps from Duncan.

MATERIALS

8½ x 11-inch green and red card stock

Poinsettia-printed paper

Red mulberry paper

Poinsettia and Christmas sentiment rubber stamps

Metallic gold micro beads

Black ink pad

12 inches ½-inch-wide red satin ribbon

Aleene's Paper Glaze

Aleene's Memory Glue

Paper trimmer

Decorative-edge scissors

Christmas Tradition Greeting

Design by LINDA BAGBY, *courtesy of Duncan*

Use black ink to stamp poinsettia image onto watercolor paper; heat set image. Color the image with watercolor pencils and paints; let dry. Carefully tear around image so paper measures approximately 3¼ x 3½ inches. Adhere photo corners to two opposite corners of stamped piece; mount onto gold card stock. Adhere paisley patterned paper to card front; center and adhere layered piece to card. ∎

SOURCES: PSX rubber stamp and patterned paper from Duncan; watercolor pencils and paints from Lyra.

MATERIALS

4¼ x 5½-inch cream note card

3½-inch square metallic gold card stock

4¼ x 5½-inch tan paisley patterned paper

Poinsettia rubber stamp

Black ink pad

Watercolor paper

Watercolor pencils

Watercolor paints

Paintbrush

2 gold photo corners

Heat tool

Glue stick

Fuzzy Garland DIAGRAM ON PAGE 92

Design by MARY AYRES

MATERIALS

Card stock: white, blue, green, yellow and red
Olive green fiber
⅜-inch gold sequin
Large star punch
Sewing machine with gold sewing thread
Instant-dry paper adhesive
⅛-inch circle punch
Rotary tool and scoring blade

Cut a 5½ x 8½-inch rectangle from white card stock; score and fold in half. Cut a 5¼ x 4-inch rectangle from blue card stock. Use tree pattern to cut a triangle from green card stock; cut a ¾-inch square from red card stock. Referring to photo, glue triangle and square to blue card stock to form a tree. Punch a star from yellow card stock; glue to top of tree.

Punch ⅛-inch holes in blue rectangle at dots indicated on pattern. Insert fiber through top hole and glue end in back; thread fiber in and out through holes wrapping fiber around tree and gluing end in back. Adhere assembled piece to card; machine-stitch around rectangle ⅛-inch from edge. Glue sequin to center of star. ∎

SOURCES: Fiber and star punch from EK Success; Zip Dry paper adhesive from Beacon.

Mitten Greetings

Design by ALISON BERGQUIST, *courtesy of PM Designs*

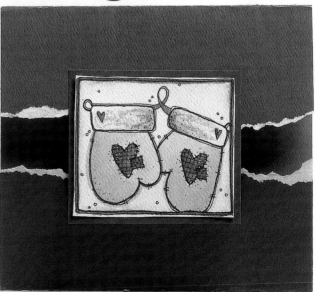

MATERIALS

Dark green and red card stock
Pre-colored mitten block
Clear glitter
Glue stick

Cut a 5½ x 8½-inch rectangle from red card stock. Measure two inches up from each short end; score and fold a line at each end so that a tri-fold card is created. Tear short edges.

Mount pre-colored mitten block onto dark green card stock; trim edges. Adhere top portion of layered image to top section of card. Apply glitter to mittens; let dry. ∎

SOURCES: Pre-colored block from PM Designs.

Season's Greetings

Design by SUSAN STRINGFELLOW

Cut deep red card stock 5 x 10 inches; score and fold in half. Cut a 4½-inch square from light green card stock; stamp pine leaf image randomly on surface using clear embossing ink. Adhere to card.

Cut patterned vellum 2 x 5 inches; tear long edges and adhere to left portion of card. Use solvent-based brown ink to stamp fruit and pine image onto cork tag; add color with watercolor pencils.

With a craft sponge, apply solvent-based brown ink to gold brads; let dry. Cut three 5½-inch lengths of red and green fibers; thread through cork tag and attach ends at top of card with sponged brads. Use brown ink to stamp "Season's Greetings" across bottom of card. ∎

SOURCES: Vellum from Chatterbox; rubber stamps from Stampa Rosa and Stampin' Up!; ink pads from Tsukineko; watercolor pencils from General Pencil Co.; cork tag from LazerLetterz.

MATERIALS

Deep red and light green card stock
Plaid patterned vellum
Cork square tag
Pine leaf rubber stamp
Small fruit and pine rubber stamp
"Season's Greetings" rubber stamp
Watercolor pencils
Red and green fibers
2 gold brads
Brown solvent-based ink pad
Watermark ink pad
Craft sponge
Glue stick

Polar Bear Wishes

Design by MARIE-ÈVE TRUDEAU, *courtesy of Magenta*

Cut a 10½ x 5¼-inch piece of white card stock; score and fold in half. Stamp polar bear image onto light blue card stock; trim around image. Add color with colored pencil. Mount image on white card stock and trim edges. Mount square on gray card stock; trim around image and adhere to card. Attach sentiment sticker below square. ∎

SOURCES: Rubber stamps and pewter stickers from Magenta.

MATERIALS

White, light blue and gray card stock
Polar bear rubber stamps
Pewter holiday sentiment stickers
Blue ink pad
Blue colored pencil
Glue stick

Star Dust DIAGRAM ON PAGE 93

Design by BARBARA GREVE

MATERIALS

5 x 6½-inch gold card
Navy blue silver-flecked
    mulberry paper
Gold-splattered vellum
Vellum tape
Holiday greeting rubber
    stamp
Small star rubber stamp
Acrylic paint: gold, bright
    gold, light gold and
    dark gold
Stamping medium
4 used dryer sheets
Gold sewing thread
Ivory sewing thread
Sewing machine
Sewing needle
Beading needle
Gold and clear seed beads
2 gold oval beads
2 gold star sequins
¾-inch gold pin back
½-inch-wide sheer gold
    ribbon
28-gauge gold wire
Tracing paper
Black fine-tip marker
Fabric adhesive
Metal adhesive
Rotary cutter and mat
Paper plate
Foam brush
Spray water bottle
Small sea sponge
Small wire cutters
Iron

Cut vellum 6¼ x 4¾ inches. Cut navy blue mulberry paper 3¼ x 7½ inches; tear long edges. Mix equal parts of gold and light gold paint together with an equal amount of the stamping medium; use foam brush to apply mixture to the holiday greeting image. Stamp message lengthwise across vellum approximately 1½ inches apart over entire surface. Repeat process with star image; set aside to dry.

Copy star pattern onto tracing paper; trace over lines with black marker. Iron four used dryer sheets on low setting; place one sheet over star on tracing paper and copy onto dryer sheet with a pencil. Stack dryer sheets on top of each other with sides even and the star copy on top; pin stack together around the outside.

Machine-sew around the outside of the star leaving the bottom between the two points open; stuff opening with gold thread between the top dryer sheet and the bottom three. Gently push the gold thread up into all the points. Once star has been sufficiently stuffed with gold thread, sew opening shut. Cut out star close to stitch line; trim loose threads.

Place star on a paper towel; spray with water until damp. Mix equal amounts of gold and light gold paint together and dilute with water; apply mixture onto star with a small sea sponge. Mix dark gold and bright gold paints together; apply this color to star in same manner; allow to dry.

Using beading needle and gold thread, loosely stitch clear and gold seed beads around the entire surface of the star. Loop thread around the surface of the star in a loose fashion while stitching; tie thread off in back once desired amount of beads have been added. Using the 28-gauge wire, thread two star sequins and two oval beads across the top of the star diagonally; twist to secure in back. Trim ends.

Center and adhere stamped vellum to front of card with vellum tape. Center the mulberry paper strip lengthwise across the front of the card; fold and adhere excess paper at top and bottom to back and inside of card with fabric adhesive. Allow to dry.

Use the metal adhesive to attach the pin back to the back of the star; let dry. Referring to photo, pin star on mulberry strip; wrap the gold sheer ribbon and thin ribbon underneath. Tie into a bow and trim ends. ■

SOURCES: Rubber stamp from Anna Griffin; acrylic paints and stamping medium from DecoArt; adhesives from Beacon.

Glimpse of Christmas

Design by LEE MCKENNEY

Cut burgundy card stock 4⅞ x 6⅞ inches; apply gold leafing to edges. Once dry, adhere to card. Push out the squares from the pre-cut photo overlay; use the stipple brush and gold ink to apply color to overlay. Let dry.

Cut ornament patterned paper 3½ x 6 inches; attach photo overlay on top of patterned paper with double-sided tape. Trim edges if needed. Attach layered piece to card. Center and place a Christmas sticker toward bottom of card; use craft glue to adhere pre-embellished bow toward top. ■

SOURCES: Patterned paper from K&Company; photo overlay from Die Cuts with a View; gold leafing pen from Krylon; stickers from Karen Foster Design.

MATERIALS

- 5 x 7-inch white card
- 12 x 12-inch Christmas ornament patterned paper
- 12 x 12-inch burgundy card stock
- 4 x 6-inch green pre-cut photo overlay
- Metallic gold ink pad
- Gold leafing pen
- Vintage Christmas stickers
- Pre-embellished small gold bow
- Stipple brush
- ¼-inch-wide double-sided tape
- Craft glue

Joy of the Season

Design courtesy of DUNCAN

Attach the house sticker toward the right portion on the white card stock; lay vellum over card stock and place the remaining stickers on the vellum referring to photo for placement. With black ink, stamp "The True Joy of the Season" onto vellum; let dry.

Place the vellum and white card stock on top of the red card stock lining up right edges; fold the left edge of the red card stock over onto the vellum. Crease well; punch two holes through all layers on folded section. Use gold ink to stamp "Merry Memories" onto ribbon; let dry. Thread ribbon through holes from front to back; cross ends over each other and run back through opposite holes. Trim ends and add glitter glue to Christmas lights. ■

MATERIALS

- 6½ x 4½-inch red card stock
- 5½ x 4½-inch white card stock
- 5½ x 4½-inch vellum
- Stickers: string of Christmas lights, snowman, snowballs and holiday-decorated house
- Rubber stamps: "Merry Memories" and "The True Joy of the Season"
- Archival pigment ink pads: black and gold
- White satin ribbon
- Clear glitter glue
- Hole punch

SOURCES: PSX rubber stamps and glitter glue from Duncan; ink pads from Tsukineko.

Old-Fashioned Christmas

Design by DEBBIE RINES, *courtesy of Duncan*

MATERIALS

Kris Kringle and holly
  leaves rub-on transfers
Evergreen and paisley
  printed papers
Red vellum
2 (8½ x 11-inch sheets)
  gold metallic card stock
6 mini gold star brads
6 inches ⅜-inch-wide
  sheer red ribbon
¼-inch rectangle hand
  punch
Adhesive foam squares
Paper trimmer

Score and fold one sheet of gold card stock in half vertically. Cut a piece of red vellum approximately ¼ inch smaller on all sides than card; adhere vellum to card. Cut evergreen printed paper slightly smaller then red vellum; adhere to vellum.

Cut a 1½ x 4¼-inch piece of gold card stock; cut a slightly smaller piece of red vellum and adhere on top. Cut a slightly smaller piece of paisley printed paper; adhere to vellum. Cut out and apply "Kris Kringle" name rub-on transfer; attach a star brad on each side.

Tear a piece of paisley printed paper approximately 4 x 5 inches; apply Kris Kringle transfer to piece. Transfer a holly leaf image to each corner; attach a star brad in each corner. Punch two rectangles approximately ¼ inch apart at bottom of piece; pull ribbon through and tie a bow. Adhere to front of card leaving space for "Kris Kringle" name rectangle.
Attach "Kris Kringle" rectangle. ∎

SOURCES: PSX rub-on transfers, star brads, patterned papers, vellum and adhesive foam squares from Duncan.

Delicate Snowflakes
CONTINUED FROM PAGE 8

Groundhog Greetings
CONTINUED FROM PAGE 11

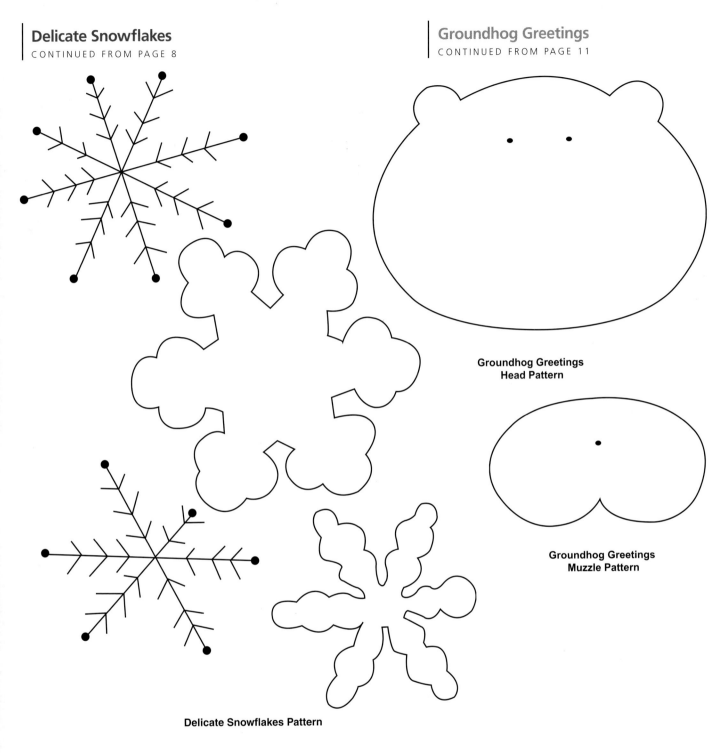

**Groundhog Greetings
Head Pattern**

**Groundhog Greetings
Muzzle Pattern**

Delicate Snowflakes Pattern

**Groundhog Greetings
Body Pattern**

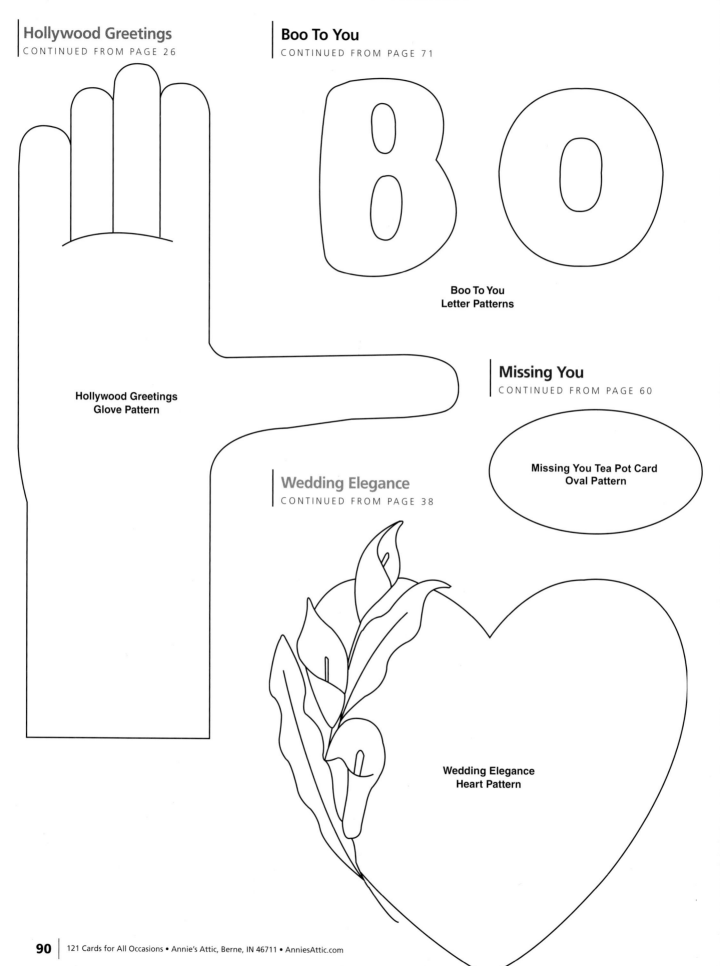

Hollywood Greetings
CONTINUED FROM PAGE 26

Boo To You
CONTINUED FROM PAGE 71

Boo To You
Letter Patterns

Hollywood Greetings
Glove Pattern

Missing You
CONTINUED FROM PAGE 60

Missing You Tea Pot Card
Oval Pattern

Wedding Elegance
CONTINUED FROM PAGE 38

Wedding Elegance
Heart Pattern

Vintage Grapes
CONTINUED FROM PAGE 65

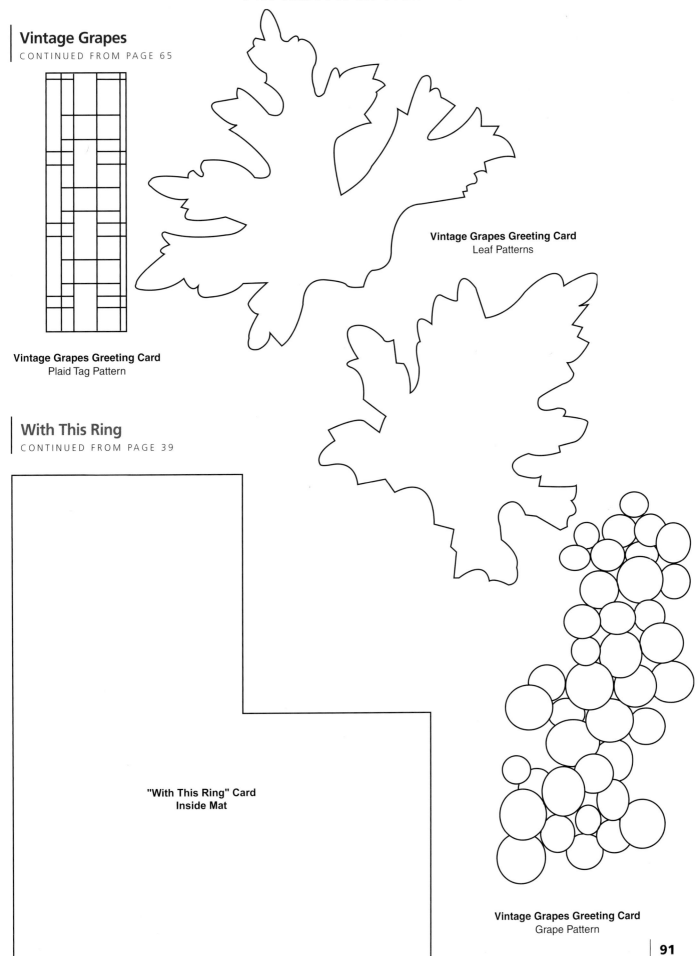

Vintage Grapes Greeting Card
Leaf Patterns

Vintage Grapes Greeting Card
Plaid Tag Pattern

With This Ring
CONTINUED FROM PAGE 39

"With This Ring" Card
Inside Mat

Vintage Grapes Greeting Card
Grape Pattern

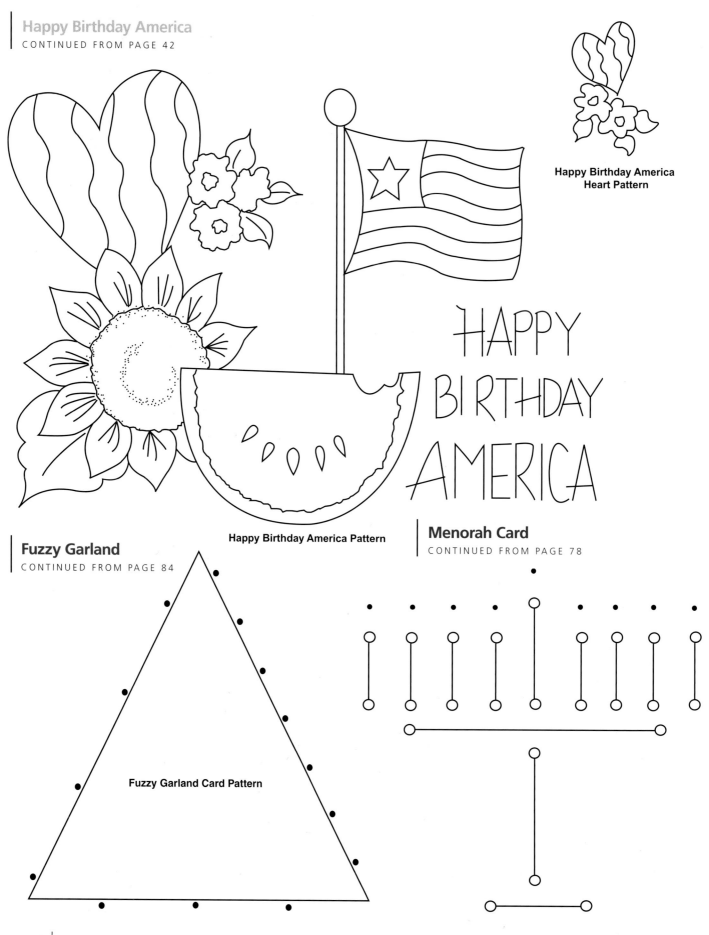

Happy Birthday America
CONTINUED FROM PAGE 42

**Happy Birthday America
Heart Pattern**

Happy Birthday America Pattern

Fuzzy Garland
CONTINUED FROM PAGE 84

Fuzzy Garland Card Pattern

Menorah Card
CONTINUED FROM PAGE 78

Menorah Card Pattern

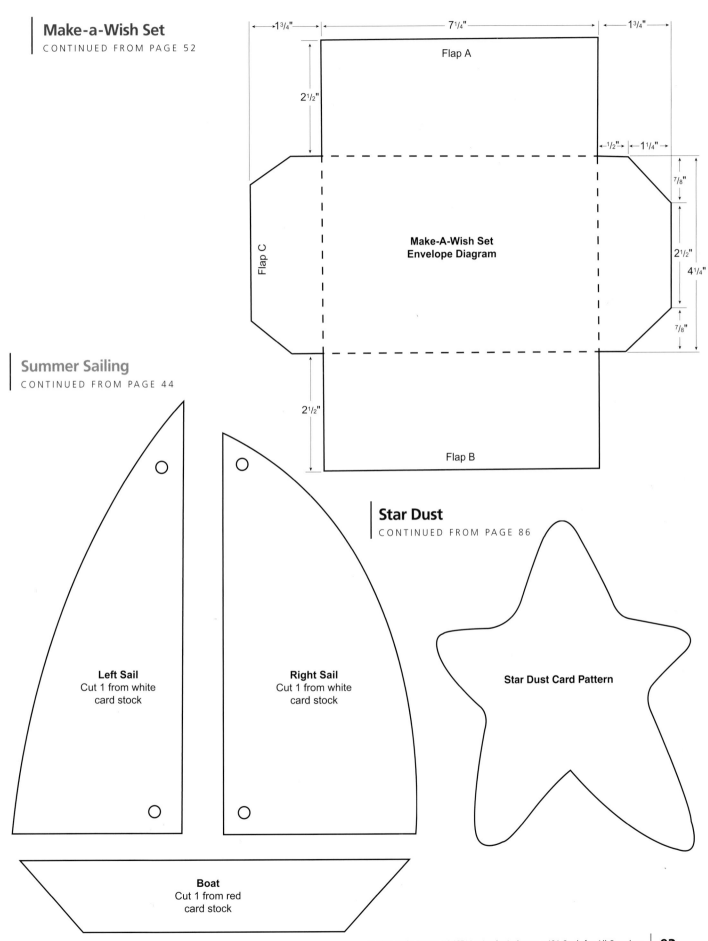

Make-a-Wish Set
CONTINUED FROM PAGE 52

1³/₄" 7¹/₄" 1³/₄"

Flap A

2¹/₂"

¹/₂" 1¹/₄"

⁷/₈"

Flap C

Make-A-Wish Set
Envelope Diagram

2¹/₂"
4¹/₄"

⁷/₈"

Summer Sailing
CONTINUED FROM PAGE 44

2¹/₂"

Flap B

Star Dust
CONTINUED FROM PAGE 86

Left Sail
Cut 1 from white
card stock

Right Sail
Cut 1 from white
card stock

Star Dust Card Pattern

Boat
Cut 1 from red
card stock

Sailboat Card Pattern

Batty Treats
CONTINUED FROM PAGE 68

Fold

Cutting lines

Cutting lines

Fold

Batty Treats Card Bat Pattern

Batty Treats Card Ghost Pattern
Cut 1 for envelope
Cut 2 for card

Trick-or-Treat
CONTINUED FROM PAGE 68

Trick-or-Treat Card Pattern

In Sympathy
CONTINUED FROM PAGE 55

In Sympathy Rose Flower Oval Pattern

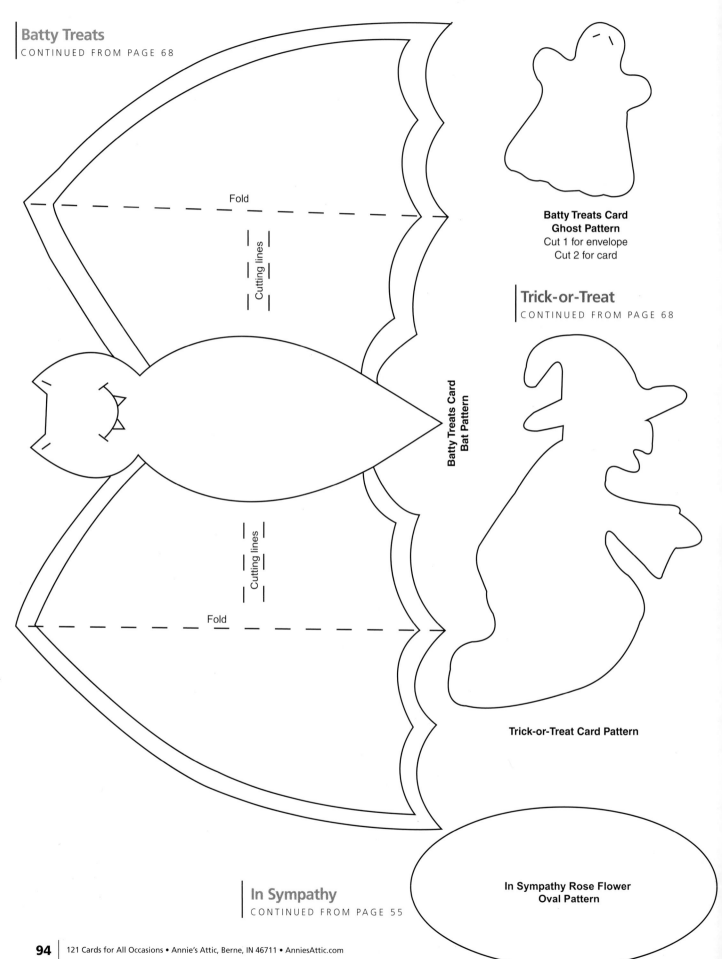

Buyer's Guide

3M, Consumer Stationery Division, P.O. Box 33594, St. Paul, MN 55133

7 Gypsies, (800) 588-6707, www.7gypsies.com

A Muse Art Stamps, www.amuseartstamps.com

AccuCut, Customer Care Center, 1035 E. Dodge St., Fremont, NE 68025, (800) 288-1670

All My Memories, 12218 S. Lone Peak Parkway #101, Draper, UT 84020

All Nite Scrapper, www.geocities.com/allnitescrapper/home

American Art Clay Co., 6060 Guion Road, Indianapolis, IN 46254-1222

American Tag, www.americantag.net

Anna Griffin Inc., 733 Lambert Drive, Atlanta, GA 30324, www.annagriffin.com

Arnold Grummer (Greg Markim), www.arnoldgrummer.com

Bazzill Basics, 701 N. Golden Key St., Gilbert, AZ 85233

Beacon Adhesives Inc., 125 MacQuestan Parkway S., Mount Vernon, NY 10550, (914) 699-3400

Bo-Bunny Press, www.bobunny.com

The C-Thru Ruler Co./Deja Views, 6 Britton Drive, Bloomfield, CT 06002, (800) 243-8419

Chatterbox, 2141 Beacon Light Road, Eagle, ID 83616

Clearsnap Inc., P.O. Box 98, Anacortes, WA 98221-0098, (360) 293-6634, www.clearsnap.com

Craf-T Products, www.craf-tproducts.com

Crafter's Pick by API, 520 Cleveland Ave., Albany, CA 94710, (800) 776-7616

Creative Imaginations, 17832 Gothard St., Huntington Beach, CA 92647, (800) 942-6487

Creative Impressions, 2520 W. Colorado Ave., Colorado Springs, CO 80904, (719) 596-4860

Creative Paper Clay, www.creativepaperclay.com

Darcie's Country Folk, P.O. Box 1627, Grants Pass, OR 97528, (800) 453-1527

DecoArt, P.O. Box 386, Stanford, KY 40484, (800) 367-3047

Delta Technical Coatings/Rubber Stampede, 2550 Pellissier Pl., Whittier, CA 90601-1505

Die Cuts with a View, 2250 N. University Parkway, Provo, UT 84604, (801) 224-6766

DMC Corp., South Hackensack Ave., Port Kearny Bldg. 10F, South Kearny, NJ 07032-4688

DMD, Inc., 2300 S. Old Missouri Road Springdale, AR 72764, (800) 805-9890

Doodlebug Design Inc., 2779 Tablerock Drive, West Jordan, UT 84084

Duncan Enterprises, 5673 E. Shields Ave., Fresno, CA 93727, (800) 438-6226

EK Success Ltd., 125 Entin Road, Clifton, NJ 07014

Ellison, 25862 Commercentre Drive, Lake Forest, CA 92630-8804

Far & Away Scrapbooks, www.farandawayscrapbooks.com

Fibers By The Yard, 2818 Devonshire Drive, Norman, OK 73071, (405) 364-8066

Fiskars, 7811 W. Stewart Ave., Wausau, WI 54401-8027

Flavia Weedn Family Trust, (805) 882-2466, www.flavia.com

General Pencil Co., P.O. Box 5311 Redwood City, CA. 94063, (650) 369-4889

Glue Dots International, www.gluedots.com

Hero Arts, 1343 Powell St., Emeryville, CA 94608

Hot Off The Press Inc., 1250 N.W. Third, Canby, OR 97013

Inkadinkado, 61 Holton St., Woburn, MA 01801, (800) 888-4652

Jesse James & Co., 615 N. New St., Allentown, PA 18102

JudiKins, 17803 S. Harvard Blvd., Gardena, CA 90248, (310) 515-1115, www.judikins.com

K&Company, 8500 N.W. River Park Drive, Pillar #136, Parkville, MO 64152

Karen Foster Design, www.scrapbookpaper.com

KI Memories, www.kimemories.com

Kreinik Mfg. Co. Inc., 3106 Lord Baltimore Drive, Suite 101, Baltimore, MD 21244, www.kreinik.com

Krylon/Sherwin-Williams Co., Craft Customer Service, W. 101 Prospect Ave., Cleveland, OH 44115

Lasting Impressions for Paper Inc. 2441 S. 1560 W. Woods Cross, UT 84087, (800) 9-EMBOSS

LazerLetterz, www.lazerletterz.com

Loew-Cornell, 563 Chestnut Ave., Teaneck, NJ 07666-2490

Lyra, www.lyra.de

Magenta, www.magentarubberstamps.com

Magic Mesh, P.O. Box 8, Lake City, MN 55041, (651) 345-6374

Magic Mounts, P.O. Box 997, 734 Fair Ave. N.W., New Philadelphia, OH 44663, (800) 332-0050

Magic Scraps, 1232 Exchange Drive, Richardson, TX 75081

Making Memories, 1168 W. 500 N., Centerville, UT 84014, (801) 294-0430

Mark Enterprises, (800) 443-3430, www.productsusa.com/mark_enterprises

Martin F. Weber, www.weberart.com

McGill Craftivity Inc., P.O. Box 177, Marengo, IL 60152

Memories Complete, 329 S. 860 E., American Fork, UT 84003-3306, (866) 966-6365

Mrs. Grossman's, 3810 Cypress Drive, Petaluma, CA 94954

NRN Designs, www.nrndesigns.com

Offray, R.R. 24, Box 601, Chester, NJ 07930-0601

Paper Adventures, 901 S. 5th St., Milwaukee, WI 53204

Paper Parachute, www.paperparachute.com

The Paper Cut Inc., www.thepapercut.com

The Paper Loft, www.paperloft.com

The Paper Patch, www.paperpatch.com

Pebbles Inc., www.pebblesinc.com

Pebeo, www.pebeo.com

Penny Black Inc., www.pennyblackinc.com, (510) 849-645-5760

Pilgrim Imports Mailable Art, (800) 571-0133

Plaid/All Night Media, 3225 Westech Drive, Norcross, GA 30092

PM Designs, 565 W. Lambert, Unit B, Brea, CA 92821, (888) 595-2887, www.puzzlemates.com

Prismacolor, www.prismacolor.com, (800) 323-0749

Provo Craft, mail-order source: **Creative Express,** 295 W. Center St., Provo, UT 84601-4436

Punch Bunch, 2819 West Adams Ave., Temple, TX 76504, (254) 791-4209

Ranger Industries Inc., 15 Park Road, Tinton Falls, NJ 07724

Red Castle Inc., www.red-castle.com

Royal & Langnickel, www.royalbrush.com

Rusty Pickle, www.rustypickle.com

Sakura of America, 30780 San Clemente St., Hayward, CA 95455

ScrapLovers, www.scraplovers.com

SEI, 1717 S. 450 W., Logan, UT 84321, (800) 333-3279

Shortcuts/Paramount Brands, 3950 Paramount Blvd., Suite 100, Lakewood, CA 90712, (866) 329-9800

Stampendous, 12240 North Red Gum, Anaheim, CA 92806-1820, (800) 869-0474

Stampin' Up!, (800) STAMPUP, www.stampinup.com

Therm O Web, 770 Glenn Ave., Wheeling, IL 60090, (847) 520-5200

Tombow, (800) 835-3232, www.tombowusa.com

Treehouse Designs, 4545 W. Bethany Road, North Little Rock, AR 72117, (877) 372-1109

Tsukineko Inc., 17640 N.E. 65th St., Redmond, WA 98052, (800) 769-6633, www.tsukineko.com

Uchida of America, 3535 Del Amo Blvd., Torrance, CA 90503

Uptown Design Co., 1000 Town Center, Suite 1 Browns Point, WA 98422

U.S. Stamp & Sign, www.usstamp.com

The Buyer's Guide listings are provided as a service to our readers and should not be considered an endorsement from this publication.

Paper Crafting Basics
Paper crafting is easy, creative and fun. Collect basic tools and supplies, learn a few simple terms and techniques, and you're ready to start. The possibilities abound!

Cutting and Tearing

Craft knife, cutting mat Must-have tools. Mat protects work surface, keeps blades from getting dull.

Measure and mark Diagrams show solid lines for cutting, dotted lines for folding.

Other cutters Guillotine and rotary-blade paper cutters, oval and circle cutters, cutters that cut unusual shapes via a gear or cam system, swivel-blade knives that cut along the channels of plastic templates, and die cutting machines (large or small in size and price). Markers that draw as they cut.

Punches Available in hundreds of shapes and sizes ranging from $1/16$ inch to over 3 inches (use for eyelets, lettering, dimensional punch art, and embellishments). Also punches for two-ring, three-ring, coil, comb and disk binding.

Scissors Long and short blades that cut straight or a pattern. Scissors with nonstick coating are ideal for cutting adhesive sheets and tape, bonsai scissors best for cutting rubber or heavy board. Consider comfort—large holes for fingers, soft grips.

Tearing Tear paper for collage, special effects, layering on cards, scrapbook pages and more. Wet a small paintbrush; tear along the wet line for a deckle edge.

Embellishments

If you are not already a pack rat, it is time to start! Embellish projects with stickers, eyelets, brads, nail heads, wire, beads, iron-on ribbon and braid, memorabilia and printed ephemera.

Embossing

Dry embossing Use a light source, stencil, card stock and stylus tool. Add color, or leave raised areas plain.

Heat embossing Use embossing powder, ink, card stock and a heat tool to create raised designs and textures. Powders come in a wide range of colors. Fine grain is called "detail" and heavier called "ultrathick." Embossing powders will not stick to most dye inks—use pigment inks or special clear embossing inks for best results.

Glues and Adhesives

Basics Each glue or adhesive is formulated for a particular use and specified surfaces. Read the label and carefully follow directions, especially those that involve personal safety and health.

Foam tape adds dimension.

Glue dots, adhesive sheets and cartridge type machines quick grab, no drying time needed.

Glue pens Fine line control.

Glue sticks Wide coverage.

Repositionable products Useful for stencils and temporary holding.

Measuring

Rulers A metal straightedge for cutting with a craft knife (a must-have tool). Match the length of the ruler to the project (shorter rulers are easier to use when working on smaller projects).

Quilter's grid ruler Use to measure squares and rectangles.

Pens and Markers

Choose inks (permanent, watercolor, metallic, etc.), **colors** (sold by sets or individually), **and nibs** (fine point, calligraphy, etc.) **to suit the project.** For journals and scrapbooks, make sure inks are permanent and fade-resistant.

Store pens and markers flat unless the manufacturer says otherwise.

Scoring and Folding

Folding Mountain folds—up, valley folds—down. Most patterns will have different types of dotted lines to denote mountain or valley folds.

Tools Scoring tool and bone folder. Fingernails will scar the surface of the paper.

Paper and Card Stock

Card stock Heavier and stiffer than paper. A sturdy surface for cards, boxes, ornaments.

Paper Lighter weight surfaces used for drawing, stamping, collage.

Storage and organization Store paper flat and away from moisture.

Arrange by color, size or type. Keep your scraps for collage projects.

Types Handmade, milled, marbled, mulberry, origami, embossed, glossy, matte, botanical inclusions, vellum, parchment, preprinted, tissue and more.

Stamping

Direct-to-paper (DTP) Use ink pad, sponge or stylus tool to apply ink instead of a rubber stamp.

Inks Available in pads and re-inker bottles. Types include dye and pigment, permanent, waterproof and fade resistant or archival, chalk finish, fast drying, slow drying, rainbow and more. Read the labels to determine what is best for a project or surface.

Make stamps Carve rubber, erasers, carving blocks, vegetables. Heat Magic Stamp foam blocks to press against textures. Stamp found objects such as leaves and flowers, keys and coins, etc.

Stamps Sold mounted on wood, acrylic or foam, or unmounted (rubber part only), made from vulcanized rubber, acrylic or foam.

Store Flat and away from light and heat.

Techniques Tap the ink onto the stamp (using the pad as the applicator) or tap the stamp onto the ink pad. Stamp with even hand pressure (no rocking) for best results. For very large stamps, apply ink with a brayer. Color the surface of a stamp with watercolor markers (several colors), huff with breath to keep the colors moist, then stamp; or lightly spray with water mist before stamping for a very different effect.

Unmounted stamps Mount temporarily on acrylic blocks with Scotch Poster Tape on one surface (nothing on the rubber stamp) or one of the other methods (hook and loop, paint on adhesives, cling plastic).

Designer Listing & Project Index